THE GREAT AZERBAIJANI POET, NIZAMI:

LIFE, WORK AND TIMES

THE GREAT
AZERBAIJANI POET,
NIZAMI:
LIFE, WORK AND TIMES

by

Evgenii E. Berthels

Translated from the Russian by Maroussia
Bednarkiewicz; excerpts of Persian poetry
translated from the original by James White

Edited by Edmund Herzig and Paul D. Wordsworth

With a foreword by Elchin Afandiyev

GILGAMESH

The Great Azerbaijani Poet, Nizami:
Life, Work and Times

Published by Gilgamesh Publishing in 2016
Email: info@gilgamesh-publishing.co.uk
www.gilgamesh-publishing.co.uk

ISBN 978-1-908531-74-2
© The estate of Evegeni E Berthels, 2017

First published by the executive Presidium of the Azerbaijani Section of the
Academy of Sciences USSR, Baku 1940. Deputy Chairman of the Presidium,
A. A. Yakubov

This edition translated from the Russian by Maroussia Bednarkiewicz; excerpts
of Persian poetry translated from the original by James White; edited by
Edmund Herzig and Paul Wordsworth; with a foreword by Elchin Afandiyev and
introduction by Edmund Herzig.

This publication has been supported by the Oxford Nizami Ganjavi Programme, a joint
initiative of the University of Oxford and Moscow State University, Baku Branch. The
Programme was made possible by the generous support and guidance of Professor Nargiz
Pashayeva. Professor Robert Hoyland was the first director of the programme (2014-16).
Professor Edmund Herzig is the current director (2016-).

CIP Data: A catalogue for this book
is available from the British Library

CONTENTS

FOREWORD

Nizami Ganjavi is a remarkable figure, not only in literature and art, but also human civilization in general. The evaluation of his work and our respect for him today do not recognize any national, racial, religious or geographical borders. A Poet, with a capital P, Nizami's work transcends the age he lived in and has remained relevant over the 850 years since. Without any doubt, it will continue to be relevant long into the future.

Nizami's writings seem to rise above the changing social structures and the great panoply of political-social development that humanity has gone through since. Feudalism, socialism, capitalism play little role when evaluating Nizami. His creative output - the five epic poems and sixty thousand lines of the *Khamsa* ('Pentalogy') as well as the lyric poems - are as topical and modern today as they were then, with a powerful artistic, aesthetic, and social-philosophical significance that continues to ring true.

A fascinating example of this can be seen in the celebrations of Nizami's work during the frightening period of Stalin's repressive regime. In 1939 the leader of the Azeri communists (and in reality the owner of Azerbaijan), Mir Jafar Baghirov, personally agreed with Stalin to hold an 800-year jubilee celebration of Nizami. It was a decision supported at the highest levels of government, but the irony was completely lost to sight. On the one hand, we have Stalin's system, which was daily laying waste to Nizami's humanist ideals in direct opposition to his philosophy that any kind of violence destroys the state, and on the other hand, those same orchestrators of the whole despotic system hold a festive celebration to herald of the great writer's ideas.

Nizami Ganjavi's *Khamsa* was created approximately two centuries after the *Shah-nama* of the great Persian poet Abdulqasim Firdawsi and took the epic traditions of the immortal *Shah-nama* to a new level. The *Khamsa* occupies one of the most important places in the development of the moral-aesthetic values that were to lay the foundation of the Eastern Renaissance. Together with these epic poem-novels his lyric poems have also played an important role in the broader aesthetic development of literature internationally.

The reader has only to take a cursory look at the geographical addresses of the *Khamsa* to understand the great width of his artistic scope: ancient Greece (the *Iskandar-nama,* whose hero is Alexander of Macedon), or the native land of the legendary ruler Khusraw, Iran (*Khusraw va Shirin*), or the Turkish, Greek, Slav, Indian, Khwarazmian, Arab and Chinese lands represented by the seven beauties (*Haft Paykar,* 'The Seven Beauties'). Separately, the diverse religious backgrounds of the heroes of these narratives point to the high level of tolerance in Nizami's world view.

The broadness and depth of Nizami's themes have been widely fêted. No less a literary figure than Goethe declared Nizami to be 'the poet of all times and nations.' His compatriot, Heinrich Heine, wrote emotionally of the poet: 'Germany has its own great poets… but who are they when compared to Nizami?'

Historical sources tell us that some twenty thousand couplets are lost to us today as a result of wars, pillages, fires and earthquakes. However, in spite of this tragic loss, Nizami Ganjavi still stands as one of the world's towering figures, alongside such literary greats as Homer, Virgil, Dante and Shakespeare. Such stories as *Khusraw and Shirin, Layla and Majnun,* and *The Seven Beauties* sit comfortably alongside masterpieces of world literature like *Daphnis and Chloe* and *Hero and Leander.*

Nizami was born in the ancient Azeri city of Ganja. He took the name of this city as his pseudonym and lived there all his life. Declining the invitations of great rulers, Nizami Ganjavi never became a court poet. His love of freedom was a distinctive characteristic of his personality and he resolutely refused to exchange his personal liberty and freedom for the prosperity of the palace.

The intended creation of a new centre at Oxford University, named after Nizami Ganjavi, is an indicator of the impressive longevity of his works. The centre's scholars and students will continue the already centuries-long tradition of Nizami scholarship among west European and Russian orientalists and historians, a tradition to which famous Azeri scholars, such as H. Arasli, M. Quluzada, A. Agayev, R. Aliyev and A. Rustamova to name but a few, have made and are making significant contributions.

This book is the work of the famous orientalist, Professor Evgeniĭ Berthels. Born in 1890, the son of a doctor, Berthels graduated in law from the St Petersburg Imperial University in 1914 before going on in 1918 to study at the Petrograd Conservatory and the Oriental Department of Petrograd (later Leningrad) State University. The 66 dramatic and complex years of Professor Berthels' life were spent in the Soviet Union. He conducted his research through repressive times and spent most of his life in libraries and archives. Able to read and write in almost thirty Western and Eastern languages, Berthels was a distinguished man of letters and focused his research on the works of Firdawsi, Jami, Navai and other Eastern writers and poets. His learning did not protect him from persecution, however. He was first arrested, without any reason, as an anti-Bolshevik in 1922, then as a French spy in 1925 and, most terrifyingly, as a German spy during the frightening period of Hitler's attack on the USSR in 1941. Each time, he was freed after several months of torture and investigation. Such personal attacks under Stalin's system would usually result in one of three tragic outcomes: the victim would be either shot, sent to Siberia or simply have their spirit broken beyond repair. Professor Berthels was forced to write denunciations (*donos*) for the KGB, which in turn led to the harassment of other scholars.

Today, we can appreciate that these denunciations extracted from Professor Berthels under duress point not to any support for the regime, but to a great human tragedy. What lives on from him now are his scholarly works, read and studied by many. Amongst them, the book you hold in your hands now. *The Great Azerbaijani Poet Nizami* was first published in Baku, in Russian, in 1940. This, the first English-language edition, is published through the Oxford Nizami Ganjavi Programme, and thanks to the vision and endeavour of the prominent philologist Professor Nargiz Pashayeva.

I close my brief foreword on the importance of Berthels' contribution to the study of Nizami with a note on the attempt to conjure how the great man might have looked in the flesh. There is no surviving depiction of Nizami Ganjavi contemporary with the poet's own lifetime, so a competition was announced for the creation of a portrait. Three great Azerbaijani intellectuals (philosopher H. Huseynov, literary critic H. Arasli and composer U. Hajibeyov, the creator of the opera of *Leyli and Majnun*) together with Professor E. Berthels were brought together for this project and, guided by the works of the poet, these four presented a brief to the artist Gazanfar Xaliqov, who used this to create a world-famous portrait of Nizami. To my mind, however, an artist's facial features, real of imagined, tell us very little - his real portrait is his work. And there exists no better key to the great man's thinking than this book, for which we will always owe a debt of gratitude to the late Professor E. Berthels. It is thanks to his prodigious abilities that we have today this invaluable portrait of the great thinker and poet, Nizami Ganjavi, a legacy for years to come.

Elchin Afandiyev
Deputy Prime Minister, Azerbaijan
Baku, 7 June 2016

EDITOR'S INTRODUCTION: BERTHELS, NIZAMI AND AZERBAIJAN[1]

Edmund Herzig

The name of Evgeniĭ Ėduardovich Berthels[2] (1890-1957) is best known among English-speaking scholars and students for his work as an editor of Persian poetry, in particular for the nine-volume Moscow *Shāh-nāma* (1960-71), which was for nearly twenty years, until the appearance of Khaleghi-Motlagh (1988-2008), the standard edition of Firdawsi's epic.[3] An orientalist of Danish ancestry, Berthels studied at the Petrograd Conservatory and Petrograd State University, where Vassiliĭ Vladimirovich Barthold was among his teachers, before going on to a highly successful academic career, including appointments in the 1920s and 1930s at the Institute of Oriental Studies of the USSR Academy of Sciences, the Leningrad Oriental Institute, and the Tajikistan branch of the USSR Academy of Sciences (while remaining based in Leningrad). During the war he was evacuated with the Institute of Oriental Studies from besieged Leningrad to Tashkent. In 1946 he was appointed professor at the Moscow Institute of Oriental Studies, and in 1950 became head of the Soviet Orient Department of the Institute of Oriental Studies of the USSR Academy of Sciences, following its transfer from Leningrad to Moscow.

13

He carried out research and published in a wide range of fields, including Sufism and Persian and Pashto linguistics, but his core interests were Persian and Central Asian Turkic literatures. His studies, editions and translations extend from Firdawsi and the birth of New Persian literature as far as Jāmī, ʿAlī Shīr Navā ī and the 15th Century. From the 1930s to the 1950s Berthels was a leading figure in Soviet oriental studies and he taught and mentored many other scholars of Persian and Central Asian Turkic literature.[4]

The Great Azerbaijani Poet, Nizami: Life, Work and Times[5], which is here presented in English translation for the first time, was Berthels' first book on a poet whose life and work occupied a major part of his research over the course of several decades. Much of Berthels' effort was devoted to editing and translating the text of the five long narrative poems which together constitute Nizāmī Ganjavī's *Khamsa* ('Pentalogy'), with critical editions of the two books of the *Iskandar-nāma*, the *Sharaf-nāma* and the *Iqbāl-nāma*, appearing during his lifetime. Berthels also wrote numerous scholarly and popular works on Nizāmī, the most important of which were published posthumously in volume 2 of his *Izbrannye trudy* (Selected Works), *Nizami i Fuzuli*.[6]

In his preface to *The Great Azerbaijani Poet, Nizami: Life, Work and Times* Berthels uses the words 'little', 'modest' and 'popular' to describe this book, though he also points out that a popular account can be written only on the basis of detailed scholarly research (p.38). If the book is small and intended for a general rather than a specialist audience, it nevertheless occupies an important place in the history of Soviet oriental studies on account of its role in the canonization of Nizāmī Ganjavī as the 'national' poet of Azerbaijan.[7] *The Great Azerbaijani Poet, Nizami* was published in more than one version and edition, almost immediately came out in Azerbaijani translation, and formed the basis for other popular accounts and textbooks on Nizāmī. It undoubtedly played a significant role in establishing Nizāmī in the affections of the people of Soviet and post-Soviet Azerbaijan. In so doing it also helped start a tug-of-war between Iranian and Azerbaijani intellectuals over cultural ownership of Nizāmī.[8] To understand the role of Berthels and his little book in this still-raging controversy, we must pause to consider the context in which it was written and published.

The book was commissioned by the Academy of Sciences of the Azerbaijan SSR for publication to coincide with the 800-year jubilee celebrations for Nizami, planned for 1941.[9] In the 1930s literary jubilees became an established facet of the promotion of national cultures in the USSR. The 1934 festivities in Iran to mark the millennium of Firdawsi[10] (which Berthels attended as a member of the Soviet delegation) preceded and may well have informed a series of 1930s Soviet literary jubilees, starting with the celebration of Firdawsi, this time as a Tajik national poet, in the same year, and continuing later in the same decade with jubilees of Shota Rustaveli (1937), the anonymous *Tale of Igor's Campaign* (1938), and David of Sasun (1939). For the intellectual and political leadership in Baku, the celebrations of the other Transcaucasian republics,

Georgia (Shota Rustaveli) and Armenia (David of Sasun), in particular, created a competitive imperative to identify and celebrate a comparable literary national hero for Azerbaijan.[11]

The larger context here is, of course, that of Stalin's purges of the 1930s, culminating in the Great Terror of 1936-38.[12] The purges claimed most of the first generation of Communist Party leaders as well many members of the intelligentsia, often for alleged foreign connections and bourgeois nationalist sympathies. At the same time, however, the Communist Party continued to sanction nation-building throughout the territory of the Soviet Union, supporting those ethnic groups that had achieved recognition within the system in developing their own Soviet statehood, their own cultural and educational institutions, and their own native languages. In parallel, the policy of *korenizatsiya* (indigenization) promoted representatives of those ethnic groups to leadership positions in all walks of life.[13]

One aspect of this process was the creation or adaptation of national histories and cultures to conform to ideological requirements, which underwent substantial shifts in the course of the 1920s and 1930s. For the non-Russian peoples and republics a master narrative of history took shape in the 1930s, one which emphasized the association of ethnic groups with their designated territories since time immemorial, the important role played by great leaders of the past, their Golden Ages and long traditions of cultural and scientific achievement, and, especially in the more recent past, their suppression at the hands of foreign overlords before liberation through Russian intervention. If the Tsarist Russian Empire was itself an evil, it was a lesser evil than whatever had preceded it because it brought progress (particularly to the backward Asiatic parts of the Empire) and because incorporation into the Russian Empire paved the way for the eventual triumph of Communism, under which all the peoples of the Union were joined equally and voluntarily in the Soviet family of nations. In this narrative the empires of the past, whether Iranian, Islamic or Turkish, which had ruled parts of what was now the Soviet Union were cast in a harsh negative light, as were contemporary pan-Turkic, pan-Islamic and pan-Iranian ideas and movements. Any suggestion of wider regional identities and cultural connections – such as Berthels' 1948 proposal that all Persian literature should be considered as a single field (see below) – risked incurring accusations of sympathy for some forbidden pan-ideology.[14] Politics and scholarship worked together in the development of the new Soviet narratives of national history and culture, but politics was in the driving seat.[15]

In the early years of Soviet rule, these policies led to a scramble among ethnic groups for recognition, status and territory within the emerging hierarchy of Soviet peoples. By the 1930s, however, the essential shape of the system of Soviet nationalities was becoming clear. In the Caucasus, Georgia, Armenia and Azerbaijan gained Union Republic status in 1936, following the dissolution of the Transcaucasian Socialist Federative Soviet Republic, while certain other ethnic groups were accorded a lower level of recognition and autonomy. If the Soviet leadership under both Lenin and

Stalin supported national development among the peoples of the Union, it was nevertheless imperative for local political and intellectual elites to exercise extreme caution in their pursuit of national agendas. There was a fine and shifting line between on the one hand officially sanctioned national development, and on the other bourgeois nationalism, accusations of which could bring a career and even a life to an abrupt end. Academics, whether in Leningrad and Moscow or in the new universities and academies of sciences of the non-Russian republics, were obliged to tread an equally fine line between their scholarly convictions and the shifting political demands of the Soviet state. [16]

In Azerbaijan the construction of a Soviet national identity, culture and history presented particular challenges. Since the nineteenth century, western and Russian orientalist scholarship had generally adhered to an ethno-linguistic theory of the origin of nations. That theory was held also by most Iranian and Turkish thinkers both inside and outside the Russian Empire / Soviet Union in the first decades of the 20th Century. In line with this, Soviet scholarship and official documents of the 1920s and early 1930s referred to the titular nation of the Azerbaijan Soviet Socialist Republic as Turks. In 1937, however, 'as if a magic wand had touched the country' (as Yilmaz puts it), the titular nation suddenly began to be described as Azerbaijani.[17] In the Soviet Union of the second half of the 1930s an ethno-linguistic understanding of the origins of the Azerbaijanis was problematic for a number of reasons. A theory of ethno-genesis which failed to distinguish the Azerbaijanis from other Turkish peoples in Anatolia or other parts of the Soviet Union left them open to suspicion of Pan-Turkic sympathies (especially unfortunate in a period when Soviet-Turkish relations were deteriorating) and without a clear enough bond with the land of Azerbaijan. The idea that the Azerbaijani people came into being only in the 11th to 13th centuries CE, following the large-scale migration of Turkic-speaking nomads into Transcaucasia during the Seljuq and Mongol periods, was unacceptable on several counts. It left them without a pedigree as ancient as that of the Iranians, Armenians and Georgians, with all of whom they were to a greater or lesser extent in competition over claims to ownership of territory and cultural heritage. It also suggested that they had not been the bearers of high cultural and scientific progress since ancient times.[18] So instead Azerbaijani political and cultural elites developed a new theory of the origins of the Azerbaijani people based on spatial or territorial rather than linguistic continuity. According to this theory, the Azerbaijanis were the direct descendants of the most ancient peoples to inhabit the territories known in various periods as Azerbaijan (both South and North of the River Aras). Their nation was a composite of Medes, Caspians, Caucasian Albanians and other ancient inhabitants of their lands, with the Turkish component as the last significant element to be added into the mix.[19]

1936-38 were the crucial years for the elaboration and official adoption of this new conception of Azerbaijani history and nationhood, and Mir Jafar Baghirov, First Secretary of the Azerbaijani Communist Party from 1933 to 1953, was the chief architect. In 1936 he commissioned a history of the Azerbaijani nation of the USSR, a first version of which was published in a limited print run of 100 copies in 1939 and in a substantially revised version in 1941, two months before the German invasion of the Soviet Union.[20] Baghirov was a keen proponent of the territorial understanding of Azerbaijani ethno-genesis, which, in claiming descent from the Medes, had the distinct advantages of making the Azerbaijanis appear a more ancient nation than the Iranians and suggesting that Azerbaijanis (in the guise of Medes) had been struggling against Persian domination since the first half of the first millennium BCE.[21] The appeal of this version of Azerbaijani history was not limited to Azerbaijani republican elites – Stalin himself hailed the Azerbaijanis as 'the obvious descendants of the great civilization of the Medes'.[22]

The new narrative of Azerbaijani national history opened the door for the adoption as Azerbaijanis of non-Turkish-speaking cultural figures who had lived in the territories of northern or southern Azerbaijan in any period of the past. Most prominent among these (and the most urgently needed in the late 1930s' race for national literary heroes) was Nizāmī Ganjavī, a poet of sufficient renown to merit comparison with established 'greats' such as Firdawsi and Rustaveli, and one who was closely associated with his home town of Ganja and hence with the territory of Azerbaijan. As early as 1934 the Azerbaijani delegate at the Soviet Congress of Writers claimed Nizāmī as an Azerbaijani poet,[23] but it was one thing to gain the support of Azerbaijani artists and intellectuals and quite another to win over the scholarly community, in particular the Leningrad orientalists, whose voices carried authority when it came to the literatures of the East.[24] As late as 1937, the first draft of an anthology of Azerbaijani poetry to be published in Russian translation to mark the start of a ten-day festival of Azerbaijani culture in 1938 did not include Nizāmī.[25] But when the anthology came out the following year, the poetry of Nizāmī was included. So what happened between the 1937 first draft and the 1938 published version to allow the inclusion of Nizāmī in the ranks of Azerbaijani poets? The simple answer is that this was the watershed year for the official adoption of the new territorial theory of Azerbaijani ethno-genesis. There was now a basis for claiming a poet who had written all of his works in Persian as an Azerbaijani national hero.

Tamazishvili gives a detailed account of the shrewd tactics adopted by the Baku leadership to 'repatriate' Nizāmī to Azerbaijan. The campaign seized every opportunity to associate Nizāmī with other illustrious names (from Shota Rustaveli to Nikolaĭ Yakovlevich Marr to Stalin himself). Azerbaijani scholars were not included in the list of editors of the anthology on the title page. Their omission immunized both the work itself and Azerbaijan's political and intellectual leadership from potential accusations of nationalism. The success of the campaign was confirmed during the launch of the ten-day festival of Azerbaijani culture which took place in Moscow, 5-15 April 1938.[26] An editorial in *Pravda* on 5 April 1938 averred that, 'Even in the age of feudal lawlessness, the Azerbaijani people gave birth to the greatest artists. The names of Nizāmī, Khāqānī and Fuzūlī Baghdādī rival in glory the famous Persian poets Sa'dī and Hāfiz. And all three of Nizāmī, Khāqānī and Fuzūlī were fiery patriots, serving foreign newcomers only because they were forced to do so'.[27] A lead article on 18 April echoed and intensified the message: 'The heroic Azerbaijani people brought forth from its midst exponents of its rebellious, manly and fiery spirit. Even in the time of feudal lawlessness, it gave birth to such great artists as Nizāmī, Khāqānī and Fuzūlī. They were burning patriots for their nation, champions of the liberation and independence of their country'. These articles in *Pravda* constituted a clear Communist Party seal of approval for Baku's claim to the illustrious name of Nizāmī. A few months later the Academy of Sciences of the USSR likewise lent its support to the recognition of Nizāmī as an Azerbaijani poet, and at the same time called for academic research on him.[28]

With Moscow's backing, the Azerbaijani leadership could now set about preparations for the Nizāmī jubilee in earnest.[29] To do justice to that occasion, Azerbaijani political and academic circles knew that they needed to enlist the support of Russian orientalists and of the Leningrad school in particular, given its pre-eminence in philological and literary studies. They recognized that Azerbaijan's own Academy of Sciences was still too weak to undertake the necessary work on the basis of its own resources alone.[30] Support for the development of the field outside Russia was already an established tradition in Soviet orientalism – indeed it was generally expected of central, All-Union, cultural and academic institutions that they would play their part in Soviet nationalities policy by helping to build republican institutions and by training non-Russian cadres – and the role of the Leningrad orientalists and of Berthels in supporting Azerbaijan's preparations for the Nizāmī jubilee must be understood in this light.[31]

Berthels led the way by adding his voice to the chorus of support for the identification of Nizāmī as an Azerbaijani poet, communicated in the most public possible way, through an article in *Pravda* in February 1939 – a clear indication that his intervention was not merely approved, but actively solicited by the political leadership. Berthels also accepted the Azerbaijan Academy of Sciences' commission to write a popular book on the great Azerbaijani poet Nizāmī (the work which is here translated into English), and again identified him as Azerbaijani in his entry for the 1939 edition of the Great Soviet Encyclopaedia.[32] These affirmations of support from a prominent figure in Leningrad oriental and Iranian studies marked another significant step in the campaign to claim Nizāmī for Azerbaijan. Later, Berthels wrote that, 'Already in 1938 it was clear to me that wholesale attribution to Iran of the whole vast, colossal Persian literature was not only wrong, but was a very big mistake. Persian was used by many peoples whose native language belonged to a completely different language system'.[33] Berthels was by no means alone of course. Another prominent Russian orientalist who participated in the campaign was A.A. Semenov, whose 1938 article bears the hardly coincidental title: 'The Great Azerbaijani Poet, Nizami'.[34]

If the public support of such a prominent scholar as Berthels was important, his February article in *Pravda* was soon overshadowed by another (in April 1939) which confirmed the support of the highest authority of all – Stalin. In this article the Ukrainian poet Mykola Bazhan recalls Stalin's words at a meeting with several writers: 'Comrade Stalin spoke about the Azerbaijani poet Nizāmī, citing his works in order to refute in the words of the poet himself the baseless assertion that this great poet of our brotherly Azerbaijani people should be ceded to Iranian literature merely because he wrote, so they say, most of his poems in the Iranian language. Nizāmī himself states in his poems that he was compelled to resort to the Iranian language because they did not allow him to address his own people in his native language'.[35] Stalin's words, as reported by Bazhan, notwithstanding the absence of any basis in anything written by Nizāmī, gave a new impetus to Baku's preparations for the 800-year jubilee, and rapidly gained widespread currency in Azerbaijan, where they were greeted and disseminated with enthusiasm by Baghirov and the Communist Party leadership. By contrast, Moscow and Leningrad scholars never mentioned Stalin's intervention in the Nizāmī debate, and neither does Berthels refer to it in *The Great Azerbaijani Poet, Nizami,* which he was writing at more or less the same time.[36]

The context for the writing of this book leaves no room for doubt that the 1930s campaign to recognize Nizāmī as the national poet of Azerbaijan was more political than academic in character, and that it formed part of a larger project to reinterpret Azerbaijani history, culture and identity on the basis of territorial rather than linguistic continuity. Mir Jafar Baghirov and the leadership of the Azerbaijani Communist Party directed this project from Baku, supported by timely interventions from senior Communist Party officials in Moscow, including Joseph Stalin himself. Scholars such as Berthels played a significant but secondary role.

It is worth pausing to consider why Berthels allowed himself to be recruited into this campaign. A cursory examination of his biography makes it abundantly clear that this was by no means the only example of his scholarship being tainted by politics. In the face of the extraordinary pressures and hazards of the Stalin era, Berthels proved a survivor rather than a hero and adapted to the ideological and political demands of the time. Zand lists a number of his works from the 1930s onwards that exhibit strong political tendencies, and he notes also the growing use of Communist Party locutions in his writing starting in the same decade.[37] According to Rodionov, Berthels 'may serve as another instructive example of how Soviet pressure worked on the Leningrad Orientalists... Arrested in 1925 after allegations that he was a French spy, he was released due to the mediation of his colleagues. But psychologically Bertel's was broken, and it seems he was forced to collaborate with the GPU by providing them with information about his colleagues...'[38] He was again arrested and released in 1941, while his son Dmitriĭ, also an orientalist and arrested at the same time, was in the Gulag from 1941 to 1948 and then in internal exile until 1956.[39] In 1948, in an article, *'Literatura na persidskom yazyke v Sredneĭ Azii'*, Berthels argued for considering all New Persian literature as a single field of study 'irrespective of the ethnicity of its authors or the precise location of its production', but this deviation towards the views of bourgeois western orientalists exposed him to the ideological attacks that were being aimed at scholars of the literary heritage of the Islamic world in Stalin's latter years and he was obliged to retract and apologise.[40] As Alisher Ilkhamov puts it:

> *Already in 1949, the claim of samobytnost' [originality (of national culture) - EMH] pronounced by local scholars was so strong that not only past 'bourgeois' orientologists like Bartol'd but even modern-day Soviet historians and orientologists, including A. Semenov, E. Bertels, and others, were blamed for succumbing to cosmopolitanism — that is, presenting past local societies and cultures as being infused by Iranian and other cultures.[41]*

By this time, the Soviet establishment had entrenched the idea that literature written in the Persian language by peoples now forming part of the Soviet family of nations belonged exclusively to them, be they Azerbaijanis or Tajiks, and constituted a separate tradition to the Persian literature of the Iranians. Literary heritage, much like territory, had to belong exclusively to one nation. In the zero sum game of Soviet cultural politics, Berthels' suggestion that Persian literature should be considered as a single field of study was anathema.

Before turning to the content of the book itself, there is one other aspect of Berthels' career that is worth highlighting. It epitomizes the transformation of Soviet oriental studies in the Stalin period, when there was a shift from lone scholars pursuing their own particular interests to a discipline organized around large-scale, politically-directed projects carried out by teams of researchers working to centrally-planned schedules and agendas.[42] The political compromises Berthels made allowed him to become one of the leading figures in this new orientalism and to pursue what he always viewed as the most important tasks for orientalists: the publication, translation and study of oriental texts.[43] As he writes in the preface to the present work,

'It is incumbent on us to ensure that as we approach this anniversary all the working people of our Union have the chance to familiarise themselves in their own native language with the works of this remarkable

poet. In turn, this requires massive research work for, although the artistic mastery of this poet long ago achieved world-wide recognition, the study of his work has been woefully neglected, as has been the study of the literatures of the peoples of the East in general, especially when it comes to popularisation' (p. 38).

Berthels recognized that a lone scholar could not undertake this 'massive work', and that it required large-scale collaboration among scholars and research institutes. As one of the most senior figures of Soviet oriental studies, he was able to launch and lead major projects for critical editions, translations and studies of such important texts as the *Shāh-nāma* and the *Khamsa* of Nizāmī. If Soviet ideology and politics placed uncomfortable constraints on the opinions that Berthels could express in his work and coerced him into collusion with the security services and betrayal of his colleagues, the resources and backing that the Soviet state put into oriental studies made the popularization and study of Eastern literatures – which seem to have been Berthels' highest priorities – possible on an unprecedented scale.[44]

Turning now from the context to the content of *The Great Azerbaijani Poet, Nizami,* the reader may be surprised to find that in spite of the intense political and ideological circumstances of its commissioning and reception, and the lasting controversy it has stirred between Azerbaijani and Iranian intellectuals, apart from the title itself, the work contains almost nothing that pertains to the debate over whether Nizāmī should be considered Azerbaijani, Iranian or Persian. The book is, as Berthels freely acknowledges, small, modest and popular, and for the most part constitutes an accessible and engaging introduction to Nizāmī, drawing heavily on the poet's own words to sketch a picture of him and of the world in which he lived.

Unquestionably it is permeated by of Marxist-Leninist ideology, for example in the emphasis on class conflict, and by Soviet nationalities policy, for example in the denunciation of the attribution of all Persian literature to and the frequent criticism of European orientalists. Other views expressed in the work, however, belong as much to traditional European oriental studies as to Soviet Marxism. Berthels' negative remarks on court poetry and the panegyric *qasida,* for instance, could have come from the pen of many British orientalists of his generation, and English-speaking readers may detect other similarities between *The Great Azerbaijani Poet, Nizāmī* and the popular works of A.J. Arberry and others writing at about the same time. Overall the ideals expressed in Nizāmī's poetry that Berthels most admires are the poet's humanism, generosity of spirit and optimism, and his attachment to his hometown of Ganja and the urban society from which he sprang. It is tempting to see in Berthels' emphasis on these ideals a response to the absence of humanity and generosity that characterized his own troubled times. Taken as a whole, the book reads not as a salvo in a zero sum competition between Azerbaijan and Iran for ownership of Nizāmī, but as a vehicle to introduce this great poet and his work to lovers of good literature everywhere. It is in this spirit that the Oxford Nizami Ganjavi Programme now offers the book to English-speaking readers for the first time.

Notes

1. I am grateful to Matthias Battis for his suggestions for readings, and to him, Harun Yilmaz and Alexei Khismatulin for their comments on an early draft of this introduction.
2. Or Bertel's in transliteration from the Cyrillic: Евгений Эдуардович Бертельс.
3. In fact Berthels lived long enough only to oversee the editing of the first two volumes, and even these were published several years after his death, but he led the project from its inception in 1954.
4. The best English-language account of Berthels' life and work is by M.I. Zand, 'Berthels, Evgeniĭ Èduardovich', in *Enyclopaedia Iranica,* Vol. 4, Fasc. 2, pp. 166-69, originally published 1989, available online at: http://www.iranicaonline.org/articles/berthels-evgenii (accessed on 16 August 2016). References to the main Russian-languages sources up to 1989 are given in Zand. A more comprehensive and up-to-date bibliography is to be found in S.D. Miliband, V*ostokovedy Rossii. XX – nachalo XXI veka: biobibliograficheskiĭ slovar' v dvukh knigakh,* 2 volumes, Moscow, Vostochnaya Literatura RAN, 2008-2009, Vol. 1, pp. 146-48. See also, B.V. Klyashtorina, 'Rossiiskaya iranistika i trudy chlena-korrespondenta AN SSSR E.E. Bertel'sa', in L.M. Kulagina, *Iranistika v Rossii i iranisty,* Moscow, Institut Vostokovedeniya RAN, 2001, pp. 69-73; B.N. Zakhoder, 'E.E. Bertel's' published with commentary and afterword by A.O. Tamazishvili, in *idem.,* pp. 163-92; A.A. Khismatulin, 'Istorii iranistiki v IVR RAN', available on-line on the website of the Institut vostochnykh rukopiseĭ, Rossiĭskaya Akademiya Nauk, http://www.orientalstudies.ru/rus/

index.php?option=com_content&task=view&id=411&Itemid=94 (accessed on 14 November 2016). Berthels' continuing importance in the field of Russian oriental studies is indicated by the inclusion of three of his works among a short list of seventeen recommended Russian-language works on Persian literature in E.I. Zelenev and V. B. Kasevich, *Vvedenie v vostokovedenie*, St Petersburg, 2011.

5. *Velikiĭ azerbaidzhanskiĭ poėt Nizami: ėpokha, zhizn', tvorchestvo*.

6. Berthels, E.E., *Izbrannye trudy*, 5 volumes, Moscow, Vostochnaya Literatura, 1960-88, Vol. 2, *Nizami i Fuzuli*.

7. On the importance of 'national poets' in the Soviet nationalities policy of the time see, Terry Martin, *The Affirmative Action Empire: Nations and Nationalism in the Soviet Union, 1923-39*, Ithaca and London, Cornell University Press, 2001, p. 444.

8. A recent English-language study giving the Iranian viewpoint is Lornejad, Siavash and Ali Doostzadeh, *On the Modern Politicization of the Persian Poet Nezāmi Ganjavi*, Yerevan, Caucasian Centre for Iranian Studies, 2012. See also the review article by Paola Orsatti, 'Nationalistic Distortions and Modern Nationalisms', *Iranian Studies*, vol. 48, no. 4, 2015, pp. 611-627.

9. Tamazishvili, A.O., 'Iz istorii izucheniya v SSSR tvorchestva Nizami Giandzhevi: vokrug yubileya – E. E. Bertel's, I. V. Stalin i drugie', in V.V. Naumkin and I.M. Smilianskaya (eds.), *Neizvestnye stranitsy otechestvennogo vostokovedeniya*, vypusk 2, Moscow, Vostochnaya Literatura, 1997, pp. 173-89, in particular pp. 179-80. The Nizami celebrations were eventually postponed until 1947 because of the intervention of the Great Patriotic War (World War II), allowing for an unprecedented decade-long build-up to the event.

10. A. Shahpur Shahbazi, 'Ferdowsi, Abu'l-Qāsem iv. Millenial Celebration', in *Enyclopaedia Iranica*, vol. 11, fasc. 5, pp. 527-530, originally published 1999, last updated 2012, available online at: http://www.iranicaonline.org/articles/ferdowsi-iv (accessed on 16 August 2016).

11. Tamazishvili, 'Iz istorii izucheniya', p. 174.
12. Conquest, Robert, *The Great Terror: A Reassessment,* New York and Oxford, Oxford University Press, 1990.
13. See Martin, *Affirmative Action Empire* and Yuri Slezkine, 'The USSR as a Communal Apartment, or How a Socialist State Promoted Ethnic Particularism', in Sheila Fitzpatrick, *Stalinism: New Directions,* London and New York, Routledge, 2000, pp. 313-47 (first published in *Slavic Review,* vol. 53, no. 2, 1994, pp. 414-52).
14. Compare the situation of the Central Asian Jadids: Khalid, Adeeb, *Making Uzbekistan: Nation, Empire, and Revolution in the Early USSR,* Ithaca NY and London, Cornell University Press, 2015, pp. 371-88.
15. See Harun Yilmaz, *National Identities in Soviet Historiography: The Rise of Nations under Stalin,* London and New York, Routledge, 2015, especially 'Introduction', pp. 1-18. As Yilmaz notes, from 1934 the Pokrovskian school of Soviet historiography was gradually replaced: 'New historical narratives were closer to romantic national narratives than internationalist-Marxist class struggles' (p. 8). On the historiography of Transcaucasia, see also Victor Shnirelman, *The Value of the Past: Myths, Identity and Politics in Transcaucasia,* Osaka, National Museum of Ethnology, 2001.
16. On the experience of orientalists during this period see Michael Kemper and Stephan Conermann (eds.), *The Heritage of Soviet Orientalism,* London, Routledge, 2011, in particular, Michael Kemper, 'Introduction: Integrating Soviet Oriental Studies', pp. 1-25 and Mikhail Rodionov, 'Profiles under Pressure: Orientalists in Petrograd/Leningrad, 1918-1956', pp. 47-57.
17. Yilmaz, *National Identities,* p. 19. See ibid., Chapter 1 'The Construction of Azerbaijani Identity under the Shadow of Iran and Turkey' for a detailed and convincing discussion of the external and internal factors that explain why this change took place at this precise moment.

18. Ibid., pp. 27-28. It is interesting to compare the equally politicized debates over language, ethnicity, culture and territory between Uzbeks and Tajiks; see Khalid, *Making Uzbekistan*, pp. 367-71, 388-89.

19. Yilmaz, *National Identities*, pp. 29-31; see also Shnirelman, *The Value of the Past*, chapters 8 and 9. On the Stalinist understanding of ethnogenesis see, Martin, *Affirmative Action Empire*, pp. 442-43.

20. Yilmaz, *National Identities*, p. 31-35; Shnirelman, *The Value of the Past*, pp. 104-05; Tamazishvili, 'Iz istorii izucheniya', pp. 174-75. More generally on Stalinism and the purges in Azerbaijan, see Baberowski, Jörg, *Der Feind ist überall: Stalinismus im Kaukasus*, Munich, Deutsce Verlags-Anstalt, 2003, especially pp. 791-830. On Baghirov see also Elchin Afandiyev's 'Foreword' to this book, p. 7.

21. Yilmaz, *National Identities*, p. 34; Shnirelman, *The Value of the Past*, pp. 105-06.

22. Yilmaz, Harun, 'A Family Quarrel: Azerbaijani Historians against Soviet Iranologists', *Iranian Studies*, vol. 48, no. 5, 2015, pp. 769-783, p. 772.

23. Slezkine, 'The USSR as a Communal Apartment', p. 335.

24. Berthels was still referring to Nizāmī as a Persian poet in 1935-36 (Tamazishvili, 'Iz istorii izucheniya', p. 178). On the comparable debates between Azerbaijani historians and Leningrad orientalists over the interpretation of the history of Azerbaijan, see Yilmaz, 'A Family Quarrel'.

25. It is worth noting that up until this point it had not been clear that Nizāmī would be held to belong to Azerbaijan at all. The prominent writer and thinker Sadruddin Ayni had staked a Tajik claim on him in a controversial collection of 'Tajik' literature published in 1928. Objections from Russian scholars to this misappropriation of Persian literature led to a ban on the work by 1930 and exposed Ayni himself to attack as a 'reactionary monarchist'. See, Paul Bergne, *The Birth of Tajikistan: National Identity and the Origins of the Republic*, London, I.B. Tauris, 2007, pp. 78-79.

26. On the place of 'culture weeks' or *dekady* in Soviet nationalities policy, see Martin, *Affirmative Action Empire*, pp. 439-440.

27. Tamazishvili, 'Iz istorii izucheniya', pp. 176-77.

28. Ibid., p. 179-80.

29. Ibid., pp. 178.

30. Ibid., p. 180.

31. Ibid., p. 180. More generally, on support from the centre for non-Russian nationalities and republics, see Martin, *Affirmative Action Empire*. On the relationship between Leningrad and Kazakh oriental studies, see A.K. Bustanov, 'Settling the Past: Soviet Oriental Projects in Leningrad and Alma-Ata', unpublished doctoral dissertation, University of Amsterdam, 2013, available online at http://dare.uva.nl/record/439902 (accessed on 2 September 2016).

32. Tamazishvili, 'Iz istorii izucheniya', pp. 180-84

33. Ibid., p. 178. It should be borne in mind, however, that Berthels made this statement in response to the severe attacks levelled at him following his 1948 article *'Literatura na persidskom yazyke v Srednei Azii'*. See Tamazishvili's afterword to Zakhoder, 'E.E. Bertel's', pp. 185-86. For further discussion of this article and its repercussions, see below.

34. A.A. Semenov, 'Velikiĭ azerbaidzhanskiĭ poèt Nizami', *Literatura i iskusstvo Uzbekistana,* book 3, Tashkent, 1939, pp. 97-109. I am indebted to Matthias Battis for this reference.

35. Tamazishvili, 'Iz istorii izucheniya', pp. 181-82.

36. Ibid., p. 185-86.

37. Zand, 'Berthels'.

38. Rodionov, 'Profiles under Pressure', p. 55. On Berthels' denunciations of colleagues and their consequences see, Michael Kemper, 'Ljucian Klimovic: der ideologische Bluthund der sowjetischen Islamkunde und Zentralasienliteratur', *Asiatische studien,* vol. 63, no. 1, 2009,

p. 116; and Denis Volkov, 'Individuals, Institutions and Discourses: Knowledge and Power in Russia's Iranian Studies of the Late Imperial, Soviet and Post-Soviet Periods', *Middle East – Topics and Arguments*, vol. 4, 2015, p. 74, footnote 17. p.

39. 'Bertel's, Evgeniĭ Éduardovich (1890-1957)' and 'Bertel's, Dmitriĭ Evgen'evich (r. 1918)', in Ya.V. Vasil'kov and M. Yu. Sorokina (eds.), *Lyudi i sud'by: biobibliografisheskiĭ slovar' vostokovedov-zhertv politicheskogo terror v sovetskiĭ period (1917-1990)*, St Petersburg, 2003, available online at http://memory.pvost.org/pages/bertelsee.html and http://memory.pvost.org/pages/bertelsde.html (accessed on 24 October 2016); see also Khismatulin, 'Istorii iranistiki v IVR RAN'.

40. See Tamazishvili's afterword to Zakhoder, 'E.E. Bertel's', pp. 182-92; Zand, 'Berthels'.

41. Ilkhamov, Alisher, 'Iakubovskii and Others: Canonizing Uzbek National History', in Florian Mühlfried and Sergey Sokolovskiy (eds.), *Exploring the Edge of Empire: Soviet Era Anthropology in the Caucasus and Central Asia*, Halle Studies in the Anthropology of Eurasia, vol. 25, Berlin, 2011, p. 253.

42. Bustanov, 'Settling the Past', pp. 25-26.

43. In 1955, in a communication to the Presidium of the Academy of Sciences of the USSR, Berthels listed five main tasks for oriental philology:

   a. the preservation and description of manuscript collections;
   b. the cultivation of philology in institutions of higher education and the training of cadres through research thesis *(aspirantura)* supervision;
   c. the urgent publication of critical editions of all those texts that have already been prepared (and the further preparation of more such texts);

    d. the creation both in the centre and in the republics of multi-script facilities to allow for the publication of ancient texts in various oriental languages;

    e. the organization of a publication series for texts held in the libraries of the USSR. See Zakhoder, 'E.Ė. Bertel's', pp. 177-78, note 21.

44. Kemper's remarks on the pressures and opportunities facing Soviet orientalists fit Berthels' case very well: 'Is it fair to demand from scholars that they stay aloof from political mimicry or outright collaboration under such conditions? We should not forget that the Soviet political support of the field also brought tremendous new opportunities for Orientalists, with some scholars emerging as acclaimed figureheads of Soviet sciences and being able to develop ambitious theories and projects' ('Introduction', p. 9).

AUTHOR PREFACE TO THE
ORIGINAL 1940 EDITION

The cultural heritage that has become available in our great Union through the fraternity of our peoples is infinitely rich. Each of us is enriched by the achievements of one's own people. We share our treasures – the accumulated wealth of the past decades, or even centuries, has become the property of millions of people. In view of these seemingly infinite riches we are faced with a difficult task, as we have had to decide which of these treasures requires our care and attention. It is worth remembering the great words of V. M. Molotov during the 18th session of the Communist Party of the Soviet Union:

> *Communism grew on that which was created by capitalism, on its best and most diverse achievements in economy, material goods and culture. Communism itself processes all these treasures and achievements, not in the interests of a higher society, but for all people and each individual. We must not spare any effort to comprehend [our] cultural heritage. We must learn seriously and deeply. We must use everything that capitalism and the history of humanity have given us, and with each brick of the edifice built by people's labour over centuries, we must build new structures, agreeable for life: spacious, full of light and sunshine.[1]*

From this cultural heritage, one of the greatest treasures might be considered the creations of the eminent Azerbaijani poet and thinker, Nizami Ganjavi, whose eight hundredth anniversary will be celebrated by the Azerbaijani people in 1941*. This anniversary will be the occasion for outstanding celebrations not only for Azerbaijan, but also for all our peoples.

It is incumbent on us to ensure that as we approach this anniversary all the working people of our Union have the chance to familiarise themselves in their own native language with the works of this remarkable poet. In turn, this requires massive research work, for, although the artistic mastery of this poet long ago achieved world-wide recognition, the study of his work has been woefully neglected, as has been the study of the literatures of the peoples of the East in general, especially when it comes to popularisation.

The task of the present little work is modest. It should show to the reader who is not familiar with Azerbaijani literature who this great poet was, in what circumstances he was writing, what his works consist of, and what is his legacy to world literature. But for all the modesty of this task, it is nevertheless not easy to accomplish, for a popular account can be given only on the basis of a previous detailed scholarly analysis.

Thus, this work had to be preceded by many long years of research, whose results I will communicate with full scholarly apparatus to the Academy of Sciences of the USSR. Here then I have allowed myself to present to the reader only the conclusions of my research, without burdening him with footnotes and long quotations.

Since at the present time not even one of Nizami's works is accessible to the Russian reader in a full translation, I thought it useful to set out the content of these works, even if only in brief. Without this, it would have been very difficult to provide a more or less comprehensible analysis of their structure. Besides, I think that in the future, when the translations that are currently in progress see the light of day, these synopses will not become completely redundant. Of course they cannot replace reading the actual poems, but they may make it easier to make them out.

This book, as I mentioned above, is intended not for specialists but for a wider public interested in the literature of the peoples of the Soviet Union. Therefore I could not go into detail, and I concentrated all my efforts on presenting to the reader the main features of Nizami's work. I am fully aware of the fact that I could only capture a very small part of the great riches hidden in Nizami's poems. Full coverage still awaits us and will not be achieved by one person alone, but will require the collaboration of many researchers. Numerous research institutions of our country will have to take part in this work.

If this book can attract attract the reader's attention towards Nizami and convince him of the necessity to acquaint himself deeper with this poet's remarkable work, then it will have achieved its aim and proved to be useful and necessary.

Evgenii E. Berthels
Baku, 1940

Note

* The Great Patriotic War (World War II) resulted in the postponement of the Nizami 800 year jubilee celebrations in Baku until 1947. In Russia, however, academics and writers celebrated the jubilee according to the original schedule: on 17 October 1941 in the Hermitage during the siege of Leningrad. See Tamazishvili, A.O., "Iz istorii izucheniya v SSSR tvorchestva Nizami Gyandzhevi: vokrug yubileya — E. E. Bertel's, I. V. Stalin i drugie", in V.V. Naumkin, N.G. Romanova, I.M. Smilyanskaya (eds.), *Neizvestnye stranitsy otechestvennogo vostokovedeniya,* vypusk 2, Moscow, Vostochnaya Literatura, pp.186-87 (EMH).

SECTION ONE

Times

Times

In the middle of the eleventh century, in the territory of the former Caliphate, which had by then disintegrated into separate, more or less independent principalities, a new people appeared: the Turkic Seljuq tribe. They came via Central Asia, through the same gateway that for centuries new peoples had traversed to make their appearance on the stage of history. The Ghaznavids, who ruled over Khurasan at that time, were unable to defend their frontiers. In the year 1040 the Seljuqs won a decisive victory at the Battle of Dandanakan. After that no-one was able to withstand their further advance. Baghdad, which was still considered the capital city of the Caliphate at that time, albeit only nominally, fell in 1055. The Caliph was forced to submit to the wishes of the new conquerors, whose forces were augmented by daily reinforcements from their native steppes. Already by 1077, in the reign of Malik-Shah, the new dominion stretched over vast territories from Afghanistan to the borders of the

Byzantine Empire in the West and to Fatimid Egypt in the South. From Iran the Seljuqs crossed into Transcaucasia, where they conquered the principalities that existed at that time on the territory of Azerbaijan, while their vice-regents gained partial control of Armenia.

Malik-Shah relied exclusively on his vizier, the famous Nizam al-Mulk, for the affairs of the State, and under his government the new dynasty reached its zenith. At the time of the Sultan's death (1092), discord arose between the Seljuq princes. The conflicts between different branches of the Seljuqs considerably weakened their power and were used against them by their worst enemies, the Ismailis. This frightening sect defended above all the interests of the old native aristocracy and fought against all the representatives of the Caliphate. At that time, they were nested in impregnable castles in the mountains, from which they sent agents to treacherously kill their designated victims. Their assassination plan targeted all powerful political actors, all of the more or less decisive holders or power. At the end of the eleventh century, the actions of its agents reached such an extent that the Seljuqs felt in danger even within their castles or among their bodyguards. The last "great" Seljuq Sultan, Sanjar (d. 552/1157), was forced to make a series of concessions and even reached an agreement with the ringleaders of these hired assassins.

The weakening of Seljuq power became even greater with the fragmentation of their inherited territory, a fragmentation that they themselves initiated. The concept of a central government according to the Sasanian Iranian model, which had still been present to some extent under the Samanids, the Ghaznavids and other entities that had broken off from the Caliphate in the ninth-tenth centuries, was foreign to the Seljuqs from the very beginning. According to their idea of power, the lands they had conquered did not belong to one single holder of power, but rather belonged to the clan as a whole, each of whose leaders was entitled to his.portion.

Thus already from the middle of the eleventh century, the power of the main Seljuq branch, called the 'Great' Seljuqs, began to become more or less nominal, and other branches sprang up alongside it in Kerman (1041), Syria (1094), Iraq (1118) and Rum or Asia Minor (1077).

The same fate awaited the provinces conquered by the Seljuqs in Transcaucasia. Arran, which fell into the hands of Seljuq princes who ruled from Barda'a or from Ganja, became virtually independent in the first half of the twelfth century under the Ildigizid dynasty. At about the same time, the Aqsunqurid dynasty gained control of Southern Azerbaijan, making Maragha their capital. Only Shirvan maintained a local dynasty, although that too was not independent, and was subordinated first to the Great Seljuq branch and subsequently to the rulers of Iraq. Because of its geographical position, Shirvan was a permanent battlefield in the conflicts between the Ildigizids and the Georgian kings, the Bagratids, who sought to strengthen their ties with the Shirvanshahs through mutual marriages.

The transfer of power to the Seljuqs was tremendously significant for the regions that had previously belonged to the Caliphate. Even though these districts inherited a system of government from their predecessors, the nature of their rule underwent essential changes. The dazzling splendour and luxury of the royal court that were characteristic of the Bukharan Samanids, were totally foreign to the Seljuqs, who were firmly attached to their clan organization. According to historical reports, the first Seljuqs were almost identical to their troops in terms of clothes and weapons. Islam, which they had only recently adopted, retained its fascination for them, and they tried to embody its ideals in their lives and to practise justice and righteousness.

Yet this was not an easy task for them. Despite all their attention to science and its promotion, the 'Great' Seljuqs up to Sanjar were all illiterate. Thus they were forced to entrust the complex governmental machine to their bureaucracy, whose power grew to such an extent that the famous Nizam al-Mulk dared to talk about himself as the co-regent of his sovereign.

This in itself gave rise to significant abuses, which expanded even more with the general use in the Seljuq system of *iqtã*, the distribution of land as a reward with the permission to collect in tax from its inhabitants a defined sum for one's own usage. The owner of the *iqtã* did not have any right on the persons, property, women and children of the population, but it must be supposed that the excess of power of the landholders was a widespread phenomenon, otherwise, Nizam al-Mulk would not have highlighted,the fact that the owner of the *iqtã* did not have any rights other than the tax in his famous treatise on government, the Siyāsat-nāma. In particular in the outlying regions, the holders of power probably abused their position relatively often, especially since the Seljuqs abandoned the previously established institution of special informants, whose duty was to keep the central government informed about the conduct of the various representatives of the administration. This supposition is confirmed by the many colourful depictions of tyranny that Nizami preserved for us in his poems.

The relationship between the rulers and the army was particularly difficult in the Seljuq period. An enormous group of nomads arrived with the Seljuqs and constituted their primary external force. It was impossible to impose on them a sedentary way of life, for it did not match their aspirations. At the same time, the necessary sustenance for them led to colossal expenditures and imposed a heavy burden on the treasury. For each tiny delay in salary payment, there was an outburst of discontent among these troops, from whose ranks gangs of cutthroats arose, taking advantage of the endless internal conflicts to go from one lord to another in pursuit of easy profit and plunder.

Hence the Seljuq period, especially in the twelfth century, was not at all calm and peaceful. Yet it is precisely this fragmentation and weakness of Seljuq authority that gave birth to a new phenomenon that had hitherto occupied a very humble place in the Near East. This phenomenon is the rise of cities, which, with the arrival of the Seljuqs, were rid of their worst enemy, the hereditary local aristocracy, and started to develop at a rapid pace.

Under the Seljuqs, conflict between peoples and the representatives of different religions became secondary. The fracturing of another order became clear, however, namely the conflict between the nobility and the merchants and money-lenders who served them on the one hand, and the urban craftsmen and poor on the other.

The astonishing works of art, for which the Seljuq era is famous, were created by these craftsmen. The architectural monuments and metalwork of this time can by no means be considered as belonging to one single people. The efforts of all the peoples gathered within the walls one or other city, with each each bringing its inherited skills and traditions, were blended together in the skilled hands of great artists into a a single harmonious whole. The flowering of craftsmanship entailed also the development of a series of branches of science. The important achievements of the famous Omar Khayyam in mathematics can be explained by the fact that his theoretical propositions were needed in practical applications.

These achievements of the urban population could not but leave a mark on its psychology. In the cities of the Seljuq period, the "spirit of freedom" was in the air. Social cohesion made itself felt in the population's ever-growing awareness of its rights. The populace demanded justice even though in only rare cases were they able to insist on it. Of course it was still long before any revolutionary outburst; the weak seedlings of change were stifled by medieval ideology. Nevertheless, even in this respect, cities achieved a new activism. Sufism was deeply interwoven into craftsmen's circles and made common cause with their secret organisations for self-defence against tyranny. Sufi sects, such as the famous Akhi, not only did not call upon their followers to endure suffering in the hope of reward in the afterlife, but urged them directly to fight for their rights, weapon in hand.

The rise of urban life of the times was reflected in a very distinctive way in its literature. If, in previous centuries, it had been possible to make a distinction in literature between the ruling élites and the written word on the one hand, and the exploited population with their mainly oral creations on the other, now writing penetrated deeply into cities and a new urban trend arose alongside courtly literature.

Outwardly, no significant changes occur in courtly literature. Moving from East to West, the Seljuqs first conquered those parts of the Caliphate – Central Asia and Khurasan – where already in the tenth century, a rich and accomplished literature had emerged in the Persian language. The new masters took over this literary heritage together with the government apparatus of their predecessors. One should not forget that court poets under the Samanids and the Ghaznavids were counted among the court administration and were a particular kind of court functionary. By preserving the government apparatus the Seljuqs conserved also the language used by that apparatus and, what is more, contributed to the expansion of this language as a literary language far beyond its original borders.

It is precisely under the Seljuqs that Persian became the main literary language of a huge territory stretching from India to Asia Minor. The Seljuqs did not contrast themselves to the local aristocracy they had displaced, they considered themselves its deputies. The absence of national self-awareness did not afford them the opportunity to put forward their own native language, as the Timurids did in the fifteenth century. The conditions for such a change were not present at that time.

Yet as soon as the potent overlords adopted this language, it set an example for the princes under their authority. The Persian language was from the start a kind of mark of those who belonged to the highest class, and it was also a necessity for feudal lords in the same way as French was for the Russian aristocracy. But as urban life developed it started to play a visible role in cities as well. It is this international language that served as the means of communication for the myriad peoples incorporated into the Seljuq state.

This explains the wide spread of the Persian written word which we observe in this period. Even in countries with an already well-established literary language and a rich literature, for example Armenia and Georgia, the influence of the Persian language made itself clearly felt at that time. Although it could not replace the local languages, its influence appeared in literary imitation, stylistic methods and lexical borrowing.

All this taken together forces us to rethink the entrenched Orientalist views on Persian literature. Until now, Persian literature was understood as everything that was written in Persian language, regardless of where and in which context the literature was produced. Hence this complicated production was attributed to Iran, which was understood to mean that political entity which bears that name at the present time. However, backward projection of our twentieth century understanding upon realities that occurred thousands years ago is of course, from a methodological perspective, entirely wrong. Persian literature emerged not only in the territory of modern Iran, and dozens of different peoples took part in its creation. If we try to confine Persian literature to the names of the authors who lived within the borders of today's Iran, all this wealth crumbles and almost nothing is left in our hands. Just as we cannot consider the Seljuq Empire as Iranian merely because it includes, inter alia, the territory of today's Iran, so linking Persian literature with this territory and turning it into Iranian literature is incorrect. If we look attentively at this literature, for instance during the Seljuq period, we shall see how it encompassed various circles: Central Asian, Khurasanian, Transcaucasian, and others. Almost no studies have followed this line of enquiry; it is complex and requires a complete mastery of the legacy that came down to us, which is something that is still far from having being fully achieved by literary scholars.

Returning to the court literature of the Seljuqs, it is worth noting that its principal and most common form remains, as in the previous period, the *qasida*, i.e. the panegyric ode, the aim of which was to glorify the ruler and, needless to say, to obtain from him a decent reward. Court poets continued to follow the lines set out by the Samanid and Ghaznavid masters. However, the weakening of etiquette and the simplification of court life is apparent, and the *qasida* loses its grandiose majesty. While the Ghaznavid poet laureate Unsuri (d. c. 431/1039-40) tried to present to his readers the ruler as an immense superhuman figure, the greatest Seljuq master, the Amir Mu'izzi, who spent most of his life in Marv, broke down this image into a myriad of tiny and almost unconnected miniatures, giving his poetry a singular 'ornamental' character. The effective force of the *qasida* fell as the role of the sovereign declined. Thus we may talk about a certain regression in court poetry, about the beginning of its decline, expressed in the reinforcement of form at the expense of content, and the transformation of the *qasida* into a luxury item, a useless, albeit beautiful, toy.

The weakening of court literature is accompanied by the rise of urban literature. This was of course under the strong influence of the literature of the ruling classes. Cities, although they started to realise their own rights, could not yet defend them. Thus they needed to make use of the language of the ruling elite as literary language, as well as their literary practices. Characteristically, however, the city took literary form as it had been in the hands of the ruling class and inserted its own contents into it, thereby exploding this form from within. The Samarkand poet Suzani (d. 1173-4) is particularly interesting in this regard, as he used the *qasida* with an ironic tone, thus overcoming its pomposity and paralysing its effectiveness. The role played by Nizami is particularly significant in this context, for the poet set himself the task of taking over, for the benefit of the city, one of the bastions of aristocratic literature, the courtly epic. As we shall see, he succeeded brilliantly in this task.

These in brief are the main characteristics of this tremendously interesting but also very difficult period, during which our great Azerbaijani poet lived and wrote his masterpieces. Nizami is the embodiment of the turbulent growth of the cities mentioned above. Only the cities of this period, and more specifically the Transcaucasian cities, could serve as fertile ground for such an extraordinary talent to rise, like the architects of the Seljuq era, uniting the traditions of the Muslim world and the artistic wealth of the Christian Caucasus. All the contradictions of this period combine in him as if by magic, and with his bold pen he depicts for us his epoch, in plain colour and without hesitation.

SECTION TWO

Life

Life

The centre of court poetry in Azerbaijan in the twelfth century was the court of the Shirvanshahs in Shemakhi. The exceptional scarcity of sources does not allow us to gather an accurate depiction of the literary life at this court. Yet there is little doubt about the fact that the Shirvanshahs followed established Near Eastern custom and strove to surround themselves with an albeit small circle of good poets, who devoted all their works exclusively to the glorification of the ruler.

The authority and head of this circle was apparently a certain Nizam al-Din Abu al-Ala Ganjavi,[2] whose name is usually linked with the Shirvanshah Manuchihr (r. c. 1122-1150). Unfortunately, the divan of Abu al-Ala has not survived. Appreciation of his work and speculation about his life are possible only on the basis of the small fragments of poems preserved in various anthologies. At the beginning of his career, Abu al-Ala enjoyed honour and respect at court. This is attested by proud lines in a *qasida* dedicated to Manuchihr:

> *"It is quite fitting if the people of Ganja are proud /Of those like me, who have surpassed all their peers"*

However the career of the court poet was full of all sorts of troubles. On the one hand, he was subject to all of his master's whims and caprices, on the other, when he was successful, he was forced constantly to ward off his enemies' attempts to slander him as favourite and deprive him from his privileged position. This was Abu al-Ala's fate.

The poet was accused of attempting to overthrow the government – an accusation which would not only have deprived him of his position, but could have cost him his life as well. In rebuttal, he said:

> *"They told the king the most mendacious speech: / 'Abu al-Ala, your closest boon companion is informing your opponents about your affairs / And revealing your secrets to your enemies'"*

Poets were often used in this sort of way by the statesmen of the time, so such accusations might appear to be absolutely plausible. We do not know anything about the state of affairs at the court of the Shirvanshahs at this period. Yet, because Abu al-Ala did not lose his life and was only deprived of his position at the court, one might think that the accusation was a slander.

In any case, in his old age, when he was 55 years old, our poet lost his patronage and uttered bitter complaints about his fate:

Although my soul, like water and flame, is fine and strong / Why do I abase myself, like dust and wind, before nobodies?

Losing the Shah's favour must have introduced wariness into Abu al-Ala's relations with his contemporaries, for he complains bitterly about them:

In this interminable life I have not found a single contemporary / Who was truthful and loyal

These complaints were, perhaps, well founded, for, in the poet's old age, one of the most terrible blows against him was struck by one of his best students, the supreme master of the courtly *qasida*, Afzal al-Din Khaqani (d. c. 1197-1199).[3] Khaqani was noticed by the experienced eyes of Abu al-*A*la. The school, which he attended under his master's supervision, quickly allowed him to join the front rank of the masters of courtly flattery. His confident mastery of all the riches of the literary language, along with an unusual courage to create new, albeit occasionally extremely risky and incongruous, comparisons and images, made Khaqani a dangerous rival for all other court poets. Although he was aware of his student's superiority in the technical sphere, Abu al-*A*la promoted him at court. At once he was noticed and deemed worthy of the highest favour of Manuchihr and his son, Akhsitan.

However, instead of being grateful for the help he received, Khaqani paid his old master back with slanderous accusations of Ismaili links, so that he could guarantee himself a unique position at court. In the end, the fate of royal favourites befell him. His rivals raised the same accusations against him, with which he had earlier demolished Abu al-Ala, and Khaqani experienced the horror of imprisonment in the Shirvanshahs' prison in the castle of Shabaran. Although he managed somehow or other to find a way to appease his lord's anger, after he was released his career was ruined and he ended his life in poverty.

The protection of Khaqani was used by a third talented poet of the time, one Abu al-Nizam Falaki Shirvani, originally from Shemakhi (c. 1108-1146). Starting his career with astrology, which like astronomy attracted a great deal of attention during the Seljuq period, Falaki obtained a position at the Shirvanshahs' court with Khaqani's support. Glittering horizons opened up before him, and he showed great artistry in parrying attacks in literary duels with such powerful masters of the courtly style as Asir Akhsikiti and Adib Sabir. But the same end awaited him too: accusations of insufficient servility unleashed an outburst of anger from the Shirvanshah, and resulted in his imprisonment in the very same fortress of Shabaran. When Falaki came out, he

... was a dead man. You could see every bone / Sticking out from my body like the letter lam

It seems that the horrors of the prison of the time caused Falaki's early death, which was noted by his friend Khaqani.

Nizami refers more than once in his poems to the dangers that were the lot of the court poet. The fate of three of the best masters of court poetry provides the best confirmation of the truth of his words.

Apart from the Shirvanshahs, the Ildigizids also maintained court poets, among whom, at the court of Ildigiz and Qizil Arslan, a fourth important poet of this period was active, Mujir al-Din Baylaqani (d. 1196). His poems have never been studied properly up to the present, yet there is no doubt about his great talent as a poet. At any rate, such an exceptional poetic talent as the famous Indian poet Amir Khusraw ranked him higher than Khaqani, praise that cannot be overlooked. However, Mujir al-Din apparently felt the pointlessness, the nullity of court poetry mentioned above. He carried out his duties listlessly. His poems speak of his reflections on the riddles puzzling his life, and joy rarely appears in them:

> *Stand straight like a reed and prefer death to life,*
>
> *For the reed offers sugar when it is alive, and music when it is dead.*
>
> *No time either to lounge or sleep, when the snake is under [your] pillow,*
>
> *No space either to idle or play, when the lion is in front of you.*

The firmament has picked up a light and wants

To plunder the treasure-house of your life.

Blow out its light with the morning breeze, for

This thief is always greedy, and the house is full of goods

Mujir al-Din's intuition was proven right. His enemies could not bear his opinions regarding the position of the court poet. One day, when the poet was in the public bath, he was set upon by hired killers and murdered.

* * *

Ganja, Nizami's home town, was built by the Arabs between 845-853/4, but its name came from Ganzak, the capital of Azerbaijan until the Arab conquest. When the borderlands of the Caliphate started to break away and become independent, Ganja became the capital of the Shadadid dynasty (in 951/2) and the focal point of the country's cultural and literary life. This dynasty succumbed to the attack of the Seljuq Malik-Shah and Ganja became the appanage of his son, Muhammad. At the beginning of the twelfth century, it remained, as previously, the capital of Azerbaijan, at least that is suggested by the fact that the palace of the Amir of Azerbaijan, Kara-Sunqur was there. We can estimate the size of Ganja thanks to reports by historians putting the death toll during the earthquake of 1139/40 at one hundred and thirty thousand. Even if this figure is highly exaggerated, it nevertheless gives a clear indication that the city was on a significant scale for the period. The earthquake happened during the absence of the Amir himself, but his whole family died in the ruin of the palace. Ganja's difficult situation at that time was exploited by the Georgian king Demetrios [I], who plundered the devastated city and transported its gates to the Gelati Monastery close to Kutaisi, where they were still to be found in the nineteenth century.

Although the earthquake was a harsh blow to Ganja's prosperity, Kara-Sunqur, upon his return, evidently invested all his effort in rebuilding the ruins and soon after the earthquake, we hear again of Ganja as the most beautiful city, not only in the Caucasus, but in the whole of the Near East. At the beginning of the thirteenth century, the strength of the city was such that in 1221, the Mongols arriving in Ganja decided not to attack the well-defended city and were content to be bought off with payments of money and silk textiles, which were one of the main products of Ganja. Only fourteen years later, during a conflict with the Khwarazmshah Jalal al-Din, who occupied Ganja in 1225, the Mongols stormed the city and, as was their habit, burned it to the ground. On the site of ancient Ganja there was no revival of population, for a new city, called by the Russian conquerors Elisavetpol, and now named Kirovabad, was built two to three kilometres to the West of the original site.

The location of the city in close proximity to Georgian lands, although it compelled the ruling elite to keep their military forces always on full alert, was nevertheless highly beneficial for its citizens, for it facilitated trade in goods as well as, even more importantly, the exchange of experience. It may be supposed, by analogy with Ani,[4] that the artisan population was highly mixed in terms of nationality, and that this favoured cultural development. The presence of the court encouraged a significant number of artisan-artists, whose artistic works embellished the life of their lord. Undoubtedly in such conditions, there was also a significant merchant stratum, functioning as intermediaries between the citadel and the city.

The presence of extensively developed crafts is demonstrated also by the presence of Sufi sheikhs, who at that time carried on their activities primarily among artisans. These sheikhs opened up the sciences and literature for the city's population.

Hence, one can talk confidently about the leading role played by twelfth-century Ganja in the cultural life of Azerbaijan. It is understandable that it became the birthplace of a poet who has the right to a place of honour in the history of world literature: the genius Nizami.

* * *

Ilyas Yusuf, better known under his poet's pseudonym (in Persian *takhallus*) Nizami, was born in Ganja around the year 1140/1. A more precise date is actually impossible, for biographical sources about him are scarce and all of the more reliable information about him is derived from his own works.

Nizami often recalls Ganja in his writings, his *nisba*, i.e. the relational name indicating his origins, is given in all the best sources as Ganjavi, i.e. from Ganja. Some European orientalists did try to link Nizami himself or his kin with the city of Qum (in Iran), on the basis of later Persian sources, but these attempts should be rejected. They referred to a line in the second part of the *Iskandar-nama*, where Nizami ostensibly remembered Qum. But this line, as already noticed by the British orientalist Rieu, is a later addition which does not belong to Nizami. Rieu's argument closely corresponds with our materials. The best and the oldest Nizami manuscript I am aware of is to be found at the National Library in Paris and dates back to 763/1360; it does not contain this line.

As for Nizami's family, we know almost nothing about it. The only information which can be asserted with relative confidence is that when he was writing *Layla and Majnun*, in 1188, his father was not alive anymore. His mother, or the 'Kurdish Lady' as he used to call her, had also passed away before then. The character of his poetry and the entire orientation of his thought allow us to assert with confidence that his family did not have any link with the feudal aristocracy. On the contrary, it was deeply connected with the artisan population of Ganja.

The family was certainly in possession of a significant income, which allowed the sons to benefit from an excellent education. Nizami's brother was also a poet and wrote under the pseudonym of Qavami Mutarrizi (Ganjavi). He, however, on account of his mastery of complex poetical techniques, chose a different path and became a court poet. I know only one of his long *qasidas,* which is interesting because each of its *bayts* (couplets) contains one or more poetic figures, so that this poem can be used as a tool for the study of poetic techniques in the twelfth century.

The presence of such a poetic talent in the two brothers is most probably due to some extent to their mixed origins. As they had already mastered two languages in their childhood, this must have enhanced their linguistic sensitivity, improved their skills in comparing points of language, and facilitated thereby the acquisition of other new languages.

One might suggest that Nizami lost his father quite early on. This is at least indicated by the complete absence of any mention of him even in the poet's earliest works. It is further supported by his saying that his mother tried with all possible arrangements to help him broaden his education and thereby obtain the means to sustain them.

How he studied and who his master was remained unanswered questions in our sources. In Ganja, there were quite a few scholars, and with sufficient persistence, opportunities for education could certainly be found. From his works, it is possible to conclude that he was familiar with almost all fields of contemporary science.

Foremost, he must have studied philosophy (which at that time was religious). Nevertheless, it is worth noticing that Nizami's knowledge in this field, in particular his understanding of ancient Greek philosophy, was significantly broader than was usual for Muslim scholars of the time.

One might think that the proximity with Georgia, where Byzantine scientific traditions were kept alive, allowed him to obtain information about subjects on which the authorities of Arab Peripatetic philosophy remained silent.

Alongside philosophy, there was astronomy (and again, it was most commonly associated with astrology). It would be possible to compile a whole dictionary of astronomical terminology from Nizami's work. An analysis of how he uses these terms shows that he was not merely concerned with embellishing the poems using rare and difficult words; rather it was a fully conscious play with the corresponding astronomic concepts, which required complete proficiency in all branches of this science. In a smaller number of places, he mentions medicine. Just as astronomy presupposed a knowledge of mathematics, and philosophy classes were always preceded by the study of logic, so in places Nizami also introduced alchemical terminology, thus harnessing the whole range of contemporary sciences.

It goes without saying that the study of all these fields was absolutely inconceivable without knowledge of Arabic. Furthermore, poetic technique was also first learned on the basis of materials from Arabic classical poetry, and hence, one can affirm with certainty that Nizami mastered the Arabic language in full.

Nizami married around 1173/4, i.e. when he was already more than thirty years old,[5] which, according to the habits of the time, can be considered as a relatively late marriage. What prevented him from getting married earlier? The answer is possibly twofold: on the one hand, a lack of the material means, necessary to pay a dowry and set up home and, on the other hand, the intense work of amassing scientific knowledge, which, when it reached the breadth comprehended by Nizami, would not have left him free time for personal matters.

His first marriage was facilitated by the fact that around 1172/3 the ruler of Derbent sent to him a young Qipchaq slave girl called Afaq. Nizami married her and fell deeply in love with her, but he was not destined to live with her for long. In 1174/5, she gave birth to their son, Muhammad, and died in 1180, when Nizami was working on his second poem, *Khusraw and Shirin*. Nizami was deeply affected by the loss of his beloved wife, and the image of Shirin, was created to a certain extent to be a memorial to this, the poet's first, love.

Here is what he says about Afaq in this poem

> *She (Shirin) was swift-footed like my own Qipchaq idol / So that it seemed to me that she really was my own Afaq*

> *A noble beauty, fine and wise / Sent to me by the ruler of Derbent*

> *Her silks were chain-mail, more steely than chain-mail itself / The sleeves of her robe were tighter than tunic sleeves*

She rejected the advances of grandees / But bowed her head to me in marriage

As Turks do, she needed to roam / And she plundered my house in Turkish style

Since my Turk disappeared from the tent / You, God, take care of my young Turkish-born darling.

The Turkish-born darling is of course Muhammad, the poet's only son, as he apparently had no other children. He transferred all his love for his wife to his son, whom he mentions more than once in his poems. His love for his son brought them very close: the poet shared with him his concerns, and let him into his poetic projects and ideas. Muhammad was a fourteen-year-old boy when he insisted that his father should work on his poem *Layla and Majnun*, which had been commissioned by the Shirvanshah. The theme did not appeal to Nizami and he did not want to accept this commission, but his son's arguments convinced him, and so, thanks to the young Muhammad, one of the most remarkable poetic works of Azerbaijani literature was created.

Left alone with a young son in his care, Nizami was forced to look for another wife who could take care of the child. It seems that this second marriage took place around 1180. Nizami never gave the name of his second wife, yet an allusion in the second part of the *Iskandar-nama* suggests that she was called Gawhar. He lived with her until 1188, when she too died. The poet married a third time, but this wife died too, when he was finishing his *Iskandar-nama*, i.e. between 1193-1201. This is how Nizami describes the misfortunes of his family life:

Once, long ago, when the heavens were kind (to me) / I was given a slave-girl even better than that one

She showed the same kindness and submissiveness / And possessed the same wisdom of mind

Her face put the moon to shame / And she captured the steed of many a king

A noble rose – my heart's blood nourished her / No man in the world was hers but me

While she made my eyes a fount of light / The evil eye took her from my sight

The plundering heavens snatched her from me / So suddenly that it seemed as though she had never been, not even then, when she had been

What can I say of the pleasure she gave to me? / May God be pleased with her.

My lot as a wordsmith is strange / As soon as I take up an old story anew,

At the same feast where I hand out the candy (of my words) / I sacrifice a sweetly smiling bride

While I was preparing the halva of Shirin / I lost the one who had made my own house sweet

When I was building a fence around the treasure of Laylì / I dropped and lost a different jewel

Now, once more as the wedding feast comes to an end / I have entrusted another bride to Rizvan

Nizami spent the last years of his life as a widower. It was already late for him to marry again, and his son was grown up and no longer needed looking after. It is worth noting the fact that contrary to the custom of his time, Nizami never married two wives at the same time, thus each marriage took place at a different time, after the death of the previous one. This might be explained by his lack of wealth, necessary for the upkeep of multiple wives, but that explanation is clearly wrong, for Nizami expressed his own views on marriage clearly. For him, a wife was the companion and comrade of her husband. She was not a commodity, which is how the feudal aristocracy viewed women. He saw woman as the mainstay, the joy of life. When a man had several wives, then none of them, according to Nizami, could be his actual friend and he would be alone and forlorn.

Through the mouth of Aristotle, he says:

Do not fritter away the harvest of your life / On all these slave-girls from the wild tribes

One spouse alone is enough for you / Since a man with several wives has no one (in the world)

Fate is treacherous, for / it has seven fathers and four mothers

71

We have seen how Nizami tried in his early years to be conversant in all fields of science. This was in truth the passion that consumed his heart, and he spent his nights chasing this knowledge, by a dim light studying the yellowing pages of old manuscripts. Yet, the objective of his quest was obviously not to be found in these pages. Even in the 'highest science' of his time, orthodox theology, he could not find satisfaction.

His quest for truth pushed him along the usual paths of rebellious minds at the time, leading him to seek truth in Sufism, among the dervish masters. Unfortunately, we are ignorant of how Nizami fell into the dervish circle and how long he spent looking for a master. It is most likely that Sufism answered his questions to a certain extent, because of its well-known tolerance, its freedom from stagnation and the orthodox routine, which was particularly characteristic of the movement in the twelfth century.

Among all the different Sufi groups and orders, Nizami quite typically chose the most audacious one, most resolutely standing up for the protection of the people of the city. According to legend, his master was one Akhi Farrukh Zinjan. We do not know who he was, as he is not described in the biographies of Sufi masters. Yet his name itself is revealing about his orientation. The term 'Akhi' (Arabic for 'my brother') is encountered only with masters belonging to the sect of the Akhi, who played a significant role in the life of oriental cities. The Akhi assigned themselves tasks, continuing the *futuwwa* movement, which had already started during the period of the Caliphate and strived to create secret organizations among city craftsmen.

Unfortunately, we do not possess any data regarding the Akhi in twelfth-century Azerbaijan, although we do have an intriguing description of this organization from the beginning of the fourteenth century. In fact, traditions were strong among these kinds of sects, and these accounts come to us from Asia Minor, very close to the Caucasus and with which significant links had developed, and therefore, it is possible to infer that this description also applies to a certain extent to Ganja's Akhi.

The Arab traveller Ibn Battuta describes the organisation as follows: "They exist in all the lands of the Turkmens of al-Rūm, | in every district, city, and village. Nowhere in the world are there to be found any to compare with them in solicitude for strangers, and in ardour to serve food and to satisfy wants, to restrain the hands of the tyrannous, and to kill the agents of police and those ruffians who join with them. An Akhi in their idiom, is a man whom the assembled members of his trade, together with others of the young unmarried men and those who have adopted the celibate life, choose to be their leader. That is what is [what is called] *al-futuwwa* also. The Akhi builds a hospice and furnishes it with rugs, lamps, and other equipment it requires. His associates work during the day to gain their livelihood, and after the afternoon prayer they bring him their collective earnings; with this they buy fruit, food, and the other things needed for consumption in the hospice. If, during that day, a traveller alights at the town, they give him lodging with them; what they have purchased serves for their hospitality to him and he remains with them until his departure. [...] Nowhere in the world have I seen men more chivalrous in conduct than they are. [...] Standing in rows in the chamber were a number of young men wearing long cloaks, and with boots on their feet. Each of them had a knife about two cubits long attached to a girdle round his waist, and on their heads were white bonnets of wool with a piece of stuff about a cubit long and two fingers broad attached to the peak of each bonnet. When they take their places in the chamber, each one of them removes his bonnet and puts it down in front of him, but retains on his head another bonnet, an ornamental one, of silk taffeta or some other fabric."[13]

This description clearly expresses how the Akhi established their own particular working community based on sharing principles. Yet the most interesting point is that, while increasing in their own material wealth, they established a broader goal to help those in need, and to defend, taking up arms, the rights of workers against the abusive power of the government. In other words, this organisation had very little in common with the other dervish orders, which built up hospices and took care of foreigners, but did not stand up against the government; they would, at best, organise passive resistance.

In fact the twelfth-century *Akhi* positions in this respect can be verified in Nizami's own writings. In the introductory part of *Layla and Majnun*, the famous 'Saki-nama' contains the author's opinions on life, recounting and his attitude towards his contemporaries. Among a range of homilies about necessary humility, respect for others' rights and selfless service of those in need, there is one particularly interesting passage regarding the dangers of self-deprecation.

For how long can one be cold, like ice / Or float dead in the water, like mice?

Like the rose, do not be soft to the touch / Like the violet, do not be two-faced

There are places where one needs thorns / Times when madness is useful

Reconciliation with every violent person, in the poet's own words, is a sign of slavery, one should not prostrate in front of the first wretch one meets:

Self-abasement damages the spirit / To suffer injustice will only make you vile

Like the thorn, carry a dagger at your back / If you want to embrace the rose's reward

Injustice and lament stie strength / A man can die of lament

There is a need, not for longing for or deploring violence, but for resisting it with all one's might. It is hence interesting to draw a parallel between the "dagger at your back" with Ibn Battuta's description of the dagger on the Akhi's belt.

Nizami's attachment to the Akhis deeply influenced all his activities. It is among this group that he developed his broad approach to humanism, and his ardent love for mankind. At the very beginning of all of his works, there is, instead of artistic impressions of political thought, active engagement with life, unsparingly revealing all of its dark sides and tracing ways to eliminate the dreadful afflictions of his society. Although Nizami addressed the potentates in his poems, he did not do it for the sake of a piece of bread, rather, he addressed them in the traditional manner of 9th century Sufi shaykhs addressing Caliphs, when the latter were beginning to turn to secular authority. He tried to teach them faith in the omnipotent force of words, that preaching is not useless and to a certain extent it can ease the fate of urban and rural workers.

When and how Nizami started writing poetry remains a mystery. Apart from his five long poems, we have one almost unstudied *divan - collection of lyric poems*. One might think that his first steps on the path of artistic creation were precisely made in this *divan*. Arguing that his first completed poem was at the same time his first poetic attempt is impossible, however. The prodigious technical proficiency in this poem clearly demonstrates that it was preceded by long exercises and the accumulation of technical skills, which would evidently be more easily gathered through shorter lyric compositions.

In any case, one can assert with certainty that Nizami was about thirty years old, i.e. in about 1171, when he achieved mastery of the poetic techniques of his time. His dazzling creativity, his great understanding of all scientific fields and his fluency in the wealth of contemporary literary language opened the door to him for a brilliant career. He had only to serve closely any prince and he would be able to fully rely on the honour and the respect of the court, as well as for financial security.

But Nizami refused this career. Stooping for a piece of bread, begging for pittances, praising people who did not perform any action worth compliment did not match his personality. It was better to live "with the small things of this world", than to be constantly fearing for his life in the "enjoyments" of the king's court.

As a mote to the sun's light / Are you to Jamshid's pleasure-dome

Forget royal estates / Since only a life on the road can make you the lord of a village

Avoid speaking of kings / Like dry cotton avoids a raging fire

Although the fire is full of light / He who keeps his distance is safe

Although candlelight inflames the moth / It is burnt if it becomes the candle's intimate

It is worth recalling here that we know more about the fate of court poets, contemporary with Nizami, and we are thus able to understand how true his words are. A precarious destiny and certain death was the fate awaiting court poets.

Nizami refused this career, however, not only for his own security. He remembered vividly the emptiness and the inanity of these elegant verbal trinkets. Not without reason, he warned his son against this career by reminding him of an old dictum in a verse: "the best among them are the most deceitful". This explains how court poetry, more than anything else, praises wild, monstrous hyperbole, exalting a man to the height of heaven, who, in most cases, does not deserve the slightest ounce of such praise. These flattering verses, according to Nizami, are empty words, which is why poets lavish them so easily:

> *Speech comes easily / To those whose verse is empty of speech*

> *Those who bring forth jewels from stones / Struggle to make the lyre speak*

Coveting patronage was for him below human dignity:

> *While you have a mouthful of bread and a sip of water / Do not dip your hand, like a spoon, into every bowl*

The efforts that people make to amass wealth are vain, for all this wealth does not enrich their life, nor does it elongate it.

> *If men lived longer the more they ate / Whoever ate long enough would live long enough*

He was proud of the fact that he did not owe his subsistance to anyone and never asked for it. Hence he says in *Layla and Majnun*:

I will not suffer injustice from anyone for the sake of riches / But I suffer injustice at the hand of toil

Such a life might seem attractive for those who love an easy lifestyle, but Nizami saw the meaning of life precisely in hardship, and in nothing else:

I only gain the reward of my toil / If my needs are fulfilled, it is through my own treasure

When one loves hardship, then hardship loves him, and this is the only way to learn about the pure happiness of life, for

After toil comes the relief of rest

Behind the apparent rigor, Nizami's life program is full of deep optimism. It is worth remembering that contemporary court poets eventually began to curse the deceptive happiness of life with particularly strong aversion, as for instance the complaints of the famous Umar Khayyam, who longed to find the meaning of life and was unable to obtain the answer to his questions. Nizami was the complete opposite of this restless soul, unable to find peace of mind. He believed in his own work, he knew why he was brought to this world and his sole desire was to honour fully the responsibilities he had taken upon himself. Nizami's strength was undoubtedly in his link with the popular masses, with the social class that began its decisive rise precisely in his time.

Probably around 1175, soon after his marriage, Nizami started the creation of his first big poem, *Makhzan al-Asrar* (*The Treasury of Secrets*). It has not been possible to determine so far the exact date of its completion. In fact, the two last verses contain such dating:

> *It was truly according to a right count*
>
> *The twenty-fourth of the first of Rabì.*
>
> *From the Hijrah this time flies*
>
> *In five hundred seventy two*

i.e. the 30th September 1176.

If these verses were written by the author himself, there would be no doubt left. In fact, however, other dates for the manuscript could be considered and one could read either 552 (1157) or 582 (1186), for the middle number can be read as any of these three numbers. The first of these numbers, five, is absolutely impossible, because this poem would have been written by a sixteen-year-old boy, who clearly could not have written it. It is true that, we know many talented poets, especially in the East who started writing before they reached eighteen years old. Nevertheless, this serious and profound creation could not possibly have been written at such a young age. This is attested by a part of the poem dedicated to old age and describing a man who already feels himself close to this enemy.

The last date, 582, seems to be slightly too late, for it would imply that it has been written after *Khusraw and Shirin*, and this would contradict the words of the author.

Furthermore, doubts about the authenticity of this date are reinforced by the extreme weakness of the verses from a technical perspective. Of course it is difficult to present a date in a particularly artistic manner, but Nizami was a great poet who did not write bad verses, and he could have found a better solution. Additionally, in the oldest known manuscript, dated to the middle of the fourteenth century, these verses do not appear, and it seems, therefore, that this is to be understood as a later interpolation.

Hence these verses should be taken with caution and the composition of the poem should be placed between 1175 and 1179. Being able to reduce the uncertainty to a period of four years is already quite good.

The poem was dedicated to one of the Seljuq vassals, a member of the dynasty of the Banu Manguchak, Fakhr-Din Bahramshah b. Dawud II (1156-1188).

Why did Nizami address his poem to a representative of the aristocracy, which he seemingly disdains?

As mentioned previously, the main purpose of this poem is to serve as an exhortation for guidance of the government. With the help of this poem, Nizami wanted to direct the actions of feudal tyranny in such a direction that it would harm less the working classes. He thus stood in front of the feudal leader on behalf of all his brothers – bitter experiences taught him often to open his eyes – and, as anger arose, he would take all reproaches upon himself. This was a great, noble purpose which could be reached only by negotiating with the potentates. Nizami saw clearly the advantages of the Seljuq over the native, local aristocracy, and their brutal stranglehold on the city. Hence, in his poem, he placed himself in the mouth of an old man presenting an address to the Sultan Sanjar:

> *Since Turkish power came into the ascent / The kingdom has been ruled with justice*

Therefore he could trust the fact that not all his advice would be worthless, and that just a little seed would fall on fertile ground to bear fruit.

His second poem, *Khusraw and Shirin* was composed under three different governments: the Iranian Seljuq Togrul II b. Arslan (1177-1194), the Ildenizid Shams al-Din Abu Jafar Muhammad Jahan Pahlavan (1174-1186) and his brother, Muzaffar al-Din Usman Qizil Arslan who was not ruling yet.

It is worth noting that such an abundance of names in one poem is an exception. I do not know a single poem which contains more than one eulogy. Moreover, it is possible to say that for the court poet adding several dedications was truly dangerous. We know very well how the shah would punish poets suspected of trying to serve another lord.

It is true that in this case, Jahan Pahlavan and Qizil Arslan were brothers, hence there was no particular danger, but with the Iraqi sultan however, considering all his links with the Azerbaijani government, it was already much more difficult.

Hence, as mentioned previously, the poet wanted to gain a salary by any means, in other words, he needed it desperately. But this time, the poet did not obtain a response at first from the 'high sphere'. No reply came from any of the addressees.

As was the rule at that time, Nizami did not have to show his creation to anyone and could give a unique copy to the one to whom it was dedicated, but since he did not receive an answer, he shared his new poem nevertheless with his countrymen. As one would have expected, it was greeted with great enthusiasm. Nizami talked about gifts that his neighbours brought to thank him for the joy he brought about. There were, as he said himself, critics, who tried to carp about this poem, about which there was truly no critical point to be made even by the most judgmental court, but there were envious mudslingers, ready to defame any beautiful masterpiece, be it the most innocent of works of art.

The reply from the government came only six years later, after Jahan Pahlavan's death in 1186, when Qizil Arslan was on the throne. He reviewed his power and having a thirty-day journey to reach Ganja, he suddenly remembered the poet. A messenger was sent to Nizami to inform him that the Sultan wanted him in his entourage.

Nizami only half rejoiced at the idea of such travel. Yet he could not possibly refuse, and had to accept the invitation. He narrated his journey in the epilogue of *Khusraw and Shirin*, which was obviously added later to the poem.

When Nizami arrived at the court, there was a party in the Sultan's tent. Rivers of wine were flowing, and *mutrib* (musicians) and singers were warming up the atmosphere.

Despite all his love for mankind, Nizami disapproved of such enjoyments. In his last poem, he affirmed with pride that never a drop of wine came to his mouth throughout all his life. This harsh stance of his was probably well known, and because the Sultan had heard about his arrival, he quickly asked for the wine to be removed and the singing and the music to be stopped. Nizami noticed and said on this occasion: Nizami's poems are sweeter than any music; music is no longer necessary when they are there.

Thus the poet found himself under the protection of the Sultan. From Nizami's own narration of the event, it is possible to understand that this encounter did not happen in the customary manner of the court. At the beginning, Nizami had to start with the usual benedictions and gracious wishes. This was the etiquette. But the rest of the conversation took another turn. Nizami used the occasion to tell the Sultan face to face that which was his aim in all of his poems: presenting his opinions on justice and equality, and giving advice to the Sultan on how, in his views, he should be exercising his power. The Sultan's reaction to this exhortation is not known. However, one can imagine that if he was already dissatisfied with it, then, according to the Seljuq practices, he would have had to show respect towards the dervish shaykh and could not simply voice his dissatisfaction.

At the end of the conversation, the Sultan asked Nizami whether he received the two villages that his late brother, i.e. Jahan Pahlavan, allocated him as a reward for *Khusraw and Shirin*. This question embarrassed the poet, as he did not know of any such present. The people of the court obviously made use of the fact that this poet was unlikely to come to court and the information about the gift had been lost somehow on the way and never reached its destination. This was very common at that time. The benefaction was given easily, but litigious people who had a position in the chancellery were unwilling to let go a little piece of their share. One should remember here the ordeal that befell the great Fuzuli about four hundred years later, when he wanted to obtain his rights to quite a small gift from the Sultan.

Nizami's situation became complicated, for confessing the fact that he had not received his gift meant that he was bringing complaints to the court, which could have had an extremely damaging effect on his future. On the other hand, it was of course impossible to pretend he had received such a gift. But the poet managed to find his way out of the trap. He thanked the Shah for his attention, saying:

I did not set this ornamented crown with rubies / For profit first of all

But my purpose in telling this sweet tale / Became an excuse for praising kings

The late king accepted what he had demanded of me / From my own property

When the sea of his life set his ship to sail / He injured not only me, but all the world

In other words, he explained the fact that he did not receive the gift because of different issues linked to Jahan Pahlavan's death. This was of course a pretext only, for Jahan Pahlavan died in 1186, and following this, six full years passed during which the poet's labour should have been rewarded. It is difficult to imagine that he thought about doing this only in the last days of his life, and waited a long time for it for no obvious reason.

Nizami concluded his answer with a polite note suggesting that the pain of the loss was softened by the rise to power of an upright ruler, i.e. Qizil Arslan. Such words forced the Sultan to correct the mistake which had been made and Qizil Arslan made an order to hand over immediately to the poet an acquisition certificate for full ownership of the village of Khamdunian, one of the Sultan's personal estates. Apparently, this specified the fact that the poet did receive not an *iqta*, i.e a right to the revenue from on a specific piece of land, but the actual land, which he could use the way that he wished.

Nizami thanked the Shah with the customary polite phrases and was granted leave to return home. Obviously, the Sultan's generosity was, however, wider in words than in reality. On leaving tent, evidently when he was out of earshot of the Shah, some "envious" person hailed the poet, maybe someone among the writers of courtly odes, and mockingly asked him what he was really talking about, when he thus thanked the Sultan. For,

> *Is a ruined village the reward for unveiling / A bride whose feet are kissed by the heavens?*

> *A village, and what a village! Like a narrow furnace / Whose length and breadth run to half a farsang*

> *It gives no profit, but eats up my finances / Its soil does not even yield a miserable half of Abkhazia*

With these verses, he obviously wanted to say that this village was located close to the Abkhazian border and prone to raids, so that half of its meagre harvest was taken by thieves.

Nizami did not expect this blow. It is true that he replied to the mockery arguing that he did not need any wealth. A scrap of land would be sufficient to subsist. Yet, his words ring somehow bitterly, when praising the 'generosity' of the governor:

> *But when he saw my tranquil kingdom / He granted to me a state worthy of the recipient*

We do not know to what extent Khamdunian's income could improve the poet's financial situation. It is clear, though, that after this journey Nizami's fame started circulating not only within cities, but in the court as well. Two years after Nizami had addressed another potentate, the Shahanshah Abu al-Muzaffar Akhsitan Manuchihr, he was asked to compose another poem. In May 1188, a horseman brought a letter to Nizami in his modest house from the Shirvanshah. The command was expressed clearly: the Shirvanshah wished that the poet would work for him, primarily to render into Persian language an Arab story regarding the unfortunate love of the crazed Majnun for the beautiful Layla. This "young fiancée" had to be adorned with "Persian and Arab dresses", i.e. Persian language must be used and embellished by the great quality of Arabic borrowings. The style was to be as refined as possible, so that it would be suitable for "the one, who leads his kin from his great ancestors" to listen to such high speech. The necessity to use Persian was underscored because the Shirvanshahs attributed their origins to the courtly Iranian kings.

The Shirvanshah's letter, as Nizami transmitted it, contains some curious lines:

> *Consider whose necklace you will set / From the jewel-box of your thoughts*

> *Our sincerity is not like that of Turks / Turkish speech is not fitting for us*

> *Noble speech is needed for those / Born of noble stock*

The command was given and the poet was left in great confusion. The theme did not attract him; it seemed to him dull, like the scorching sun of the Arab desert. Help came from the young Muhammad who was already fourteen years old. He convinced his father that on the basis of this theme, a story about love, Nizami could revive this legend and create a masterpiece that would be worth his notoriety. On the other hand, he was dangerously playing with his relationship with the Shirvanshah. Reluctantly, Nizami started gathering his materials. The more he studied the topic, the more inspired he became. Thus the work went on quickly.

As I sought out these fine wares / My feet did not slip a hair's breadth

I composed and my heart replied / I dug and the spring flowed

The command was given in May, but on 30 Rajab 584, i.e. 24 September 1188, the last line was already written. Nizami said that if other things had not distracted him, he would have finished it in fourteen days.

Obviously, Nizami did not have the slightest wish to present himself under the 'spotlight' gaze of the potentate. He did not go to the Shirvanshah, but sent the poem with his son, who had requested of his father that he be responsible for it. He was dreaming of a career as a court poet and he wanted to get closer to Akhsitan's son, Manuchihr. This is why the father brought into the poem an appeal to the young prince, whom he asked not to neglect Muhammad, but to allocate him a permanent salary.

We do not know how the poem and the messenger were received in Shirvan. Since ten years later, we encounter Muhammad again in the house of his father, it is obvious that no position was given to him at the Shirvanshah's court. Most probably, it turned out that Manuchihr did not inherit his father's throne for reasons we do not know and Akhsitan succeeded his brother, Shahanshah b. Manuchir. Unfortunately, Akhsitan's date of death is known only approximately. He died between 1194 and 1204. If the date of his death was closer to 1194, then it would be logical that Muhammad would be back in Ganja, running away from the unrest that follows a Shah's death, when his kin would start a desperate struggle for the throne.

In any case, in the wider circles of poetry lovers, the success of this poem was particularly impressive. This is visible in the surprising numbers of copies of the poem, which spread from the Near East to India. It is true that the versions we have are dated to about a hundred years or more after Nizami's life. Yet, in view of the poet's own words, those versions that do not reach us, started being spread during his lifetime already. At first, it was not due to his amazing creativity, as much as to the effort to steal from him his successful methods, his comparisons, etc. The poet complained he had a scribe who robbed him and created a pathetic parody of his great masterpiece. He comforted himself with words alone:

An ape can do everything that men do / The stars are reflected in a muddy pool

His son left, and Nizami's large house became even more quiet. The poet said that he barely locked the doors of the house. He shut himself in his work for weeks without stopping, immersed in studying old chronicles and reflecting upon the fate of his country.

After eight years, another royal messenger arrived at the poet's house. The governor Maragha the Aqsunqurid Ala al-Din Kurpa Arslan (1174-1207) asked Nizami to immortalise his name in a new composition. The theme did not matter, his concern was

That your magic should ensnare / And your fantastic play capture sorcerers

Nizami did not immediately find the right theme. He apparently decided to turn again to the old Iranian chronicles. He leafed through them for a long time, his attention being caught by the Arabic sources, but

A quick-witted poet had come before me / Correctly making verse of everything

In other words, Nizami held the opinion that all the themes in the history of Iran were already fully explored by the great Firdawsi. Nevertheless, notwithstanding this conclusion, he found a field which could be worked on and shown in a new light. It seems that the cycle of legends about the popular hero of the Near East, the Sasanian Bahram Gur, had not been exploited exhaustively, and Nizami could base his new creation on unused old narratives. He described this as follows:

> *From those fragments, like a master jeweller / I polished this treasure*

In fact, as we have seen before, the links between Nizami's and Firdawsi's poems are quite weak. One cannot cannot talk about dependency here, and our great poet was always able to use a theme for his own purposes.

The poem was given the name of "Haft Paykar". This can be translated in two ways. The first translation that comes to mind is the "Seven Portraits", but metaphorically it could be rendered as the "Seven Beauties". I am tempted to think that this ambiguity was created on purpose, for both titles match closely the theme of the poem. It was finished on 14 Ramadan 593, i.e. 31 July 1197. In other words, the poet was already at that time fifty-six years old. Nevertheless, his age cannot be seen between the lines of this poem. It is possible to affirm that, in the refinement and brightness of its images, this poem eclipsed all his previous creations. This outstanding level of work can be explained by the fact that the poet drew more systematically from the infinite source of perpetual scenes of folklore.

It is possible to think that work on this poem might have been in parallel with the composition of his last poem, *Iskandar-nama*, or the "Poem on Alexander (of

Macedonia)". Establishing the completion date of this poem is somewhat difficult, however. This date is not mentioned in the poem. The mention that his son was seventeen years old indicates that the composition had been started already in 587/1191. The dating question is made more complicated through the presence of two dedications. The first part goes to Nasr al-Din Abu-Bakr Bishkin, but it is not clear who this governor was: whether he was the son of Jihan Pahlavan, who ruled between 1191 and 1210, or the *malik* (ruler) of the Ahar region, who was of Georgian descent. In the second part, this name is repeated, but it ends with an address to the Sultan Izz al-Din Mas'ud.

Chronologically, this can only be the Zangid ruler of Mosul, Izz al-Din Mas'ud I (1180-1193), for Mas'ud II b. Arslan Came to the throne in 1211, when Nizami had already passed away. This is further supported by the poet's mention that he was then already sixty years old. Sixty lunar years correspond to fifty eight solar years, two and a half months, which brings us to around 1200 as a possible date.

Addressing the contradictions which appear here, if we suppose that the composition of this poem, Nizami's longest masterpiece, took longer, perhaps about ten years, and that the poem was already dedicated to several rulers, it certainly requires more study.

The unusual presence of two dedications, which furthermore refer to members of different lineages, who do not belong to the same dynasty, indicates that with regards to this poem, Nizami was encountering some difficulty. In the second part of the poem he explains that some governor or other had demanded, that he dedicate the composition to him, threatening him with reprisal if he refused. This appears in the following verses:

> *Saying: 'Give us this jewel that illuminates the night /*
> *Or else quit this garden'*

In other words, if he refused, he would be exiled. Who could have expressed such a threat? The governor of Mosul did not have any power over Ganja. It is difficult to think that the governor of Ahar could interfere in Northern Azerbaijan. The only interpretation remaining is that it came from the Ildigizids who could always extend their power over the inhabitants of this city.

Wherever this threat came from, it appears clearly that the last years of Nizami's life were anything but pleasurable. He said:

> *Everything I attempt ends in grief / Yet I have no*
> *companion in my grief, no friend to relieve it*

At the end of the poem, he refers to his own domestic affairs:

> *If I cannot feast on kebabs of onager sirloin / Then nor*
> *do I fear the retribution of the grave*
>
> *And if I have no fine sweets before me / Then I will*
> *make pure brains the source of my strength*

And if the fat of my brain has dried up / I will make my soul run without fat, like a candle

Since my body has no bread on which to live / Like a drum, I will not be broken when struck

In other words, he did not have stores, and if, perhaps, the poet was not actually hungry, there was no occasion to speak of comforts. On top of everything, Ganja was shaken by a terrible earthquake that Nizami described as follows:

The cities of the world disappeared / in that earthquake which rent the sky

Such a tremor struck the plains and the mountains / That the dust reached Heaven's gates

The earth tottered, like the sky / Forced to turn summersaults through Fate's games

A blast sounded on the Last Trumpet / And the Fish fell from the Cow's back

The chains of the heavens were undone / And the joints of the earth were split

On Saturday evening Ganja was forgotten / So much treasure was scattered to the winds that day

So many women and men, young and old were lost / That nothing could be heard but weeping

All these issues taken together forced Nizami to seek support from the authorities. But, whereas in the past when addressing them, he did not go himself and sent just his composition in order not to humiliate himself in front of the nobles, this time he could not go because of his old age. He said:

Since my hands and feet cannot aid me / In finding refuge in Heaven's cradle

It is better to send one's soul to the grave's cradle / Than to shovel dark earth

But he did not want to send his son to remain in Mosul. He asks:

Return him to me from beside you, such that / His courtesy is greater than I could have hoped

My speech has now reached an end / The rest you know, do what you think is fit

This shows too well that it had become difficult for the old man to live without his son, and he needed his help and his support.

As before, we do not know what Muhammad managed to obtain from his trip. There is complete silence regarding the end of the poet's life. This is not surprising. In fact, most of the collections of poets' biographies entail either court poets, or Sufi shaykhs. Nizami could not be included within the first category; his relationship with the potentates is quite distinctly described in his work and manoeuvring into this group was not possible. As for the second category of

Anushiravan and his vizier listening to the song of the two owls.

Shirin's friend shows her the portrait of Khusraw.

Majnun in the desert, surrounded by beasts.

Khusraw encounters Shirin at the spring.

4

Bahram hunting.

The images in this plate section are the same images included, reproduced in monocolour, in the original Russian edition of this book. The captions are translations of Berthels' Russian captions.

biographies, they seem to have gathered god-fearing people, comprising collections that devote all their attention to the orders advocating Islamic orthodoxy. Such dangerous organisations like the Akhi, if they were to have their own documents, would surely also see themselves as the guardians of the faith, but these documents have not been preserved.

One of the first copies of the *Iskandar-nama* contains an addition where it is stated that Nizami finished it in 1203. This year is usually taken as the date for his death, although some sources point to earlier dates, 1194 and 1195. Preference goes to the first date, however, because none of the earlier dates can possibly agree with the indications given by the poet himself, as mentioned above.

Such was the life of this artistic genius. It passed quietly, without any particularly striking events. All his wealth was concentrated in himself, and he shared this wealth broadly and generously through his immortal creations. And if his fame went far beyond the Near East, spreading outside the frontiers of the 'Muslim world', into neighbouring Christian Georgia,[14] it is because his countrymen, who knew his opinions on life, his passionate love for human beings and his hope to help all those in need, were united around his memory which created a sense of holiness.

Hence his grave, which is located on the site of ancient Ganja, some kilometres from Kirovabad, became a pilgrimage destination. People visit it, seeking consolation from their pains, just as in the past, during the poet's lifetime; they would come to him to benefit from his wise advice.

And so the memory of this great poet lived on. And with it, lived and still live to this day immortal creations. More than seven hundred years later, people still read his works, and every century, every epoch has discovered them anew and has found new riches in them. Now that classical literature has become the property of all the working classes it has received new life, and have revealed themselves to all in their full glory, and have proved the poet right, when he said in his very first poem:

The explanation of speech is more than speech

While there is speech, may it be spoken of / May speech revitalise Nizami's name

SECTION THREE

Work

Work

In this short introduction, we have covered the poet's life and his times. In the second part of this work I shall turn our attention towards a study of the poet's art. The aim is not to provide an exhaustive analysis. Presenting all of its wealth is beyond the potential of one individual – especially now, when our study of Nizami has just started, it simply cannot be achieved.

My task is much more humble. Because Nizami's work has not been translated into the language of our great nation, and remains thus confined to a very narrow circle of readers, we shall therefore try to: 1) broadly describe its content, 2) show its links to the previous literary creations and, 3) highlight its significance on a social and artistic level. Hence, lay readers will have the opportunity to gain an impression of the importance and the position of Nizami within the artistic creations of the peoples of the USSR, while textual specialists will accustom themselves with the characteristic style of this poet, and the difficulties they encounter in mastering the text will be relieved to some extent.

Work: The Treasury of Secrets

Nizami's first great work was composed when he was already in adulthood. It is possible to suggest that this was due to an extensive phase of preparation, specifically in poetry. This is the only explanation for the prodigious technical proficiency, which differentiates every line of this poem, called by the author *Makhzan al-asrar*, which can be translated as *The Treasury of Secrets*.

The inspiration for this poem came from the work of the Ghaznavid poet Majdud Sanai (d. ca. 1141-1181), called *Hadiqat al-haqiqa* (*The Garden of Truth*). Nizami talked about it as follow:

> *Two works have come from two famous places / Both signed and sealed by two Bahramshahs*

These words show that Sanai's poems were dedicated to Bahramshah (1118-1152), and Nizami's poems were addressed to Arzinjan Bahramshah. The 'famous places' stand for the poet himself and Sanai.

Notwithstanding this link, Nizami changed the metre, choosing the so-called 'sari', a structure which can be schematised as follow:

$$- \cup \cup - | - \cup \cup - | - \cup -$$

The horizontal lines represent long syllables, the sign [$\cup$] the short syllable, while the vertical lines mark the separation between the feet.

Working on the premise that Sanai's poem represents some kind of codex of Sufi mystical teaching, European scholars have interpreted Nizami's poem as a Sufi mystical treatise and have not paid particular attention to it, considering it interesting only for people versed in the study of religion and philosophy of the Near East.

However, a close study of this poem suggests that it is not possible to follow such a narrow interpretation. It is true that Nizami gave his poem the appearance of a Sufi work,: its introductory sections have a pronounced mystical flavour, and its twenty main sections have headings including terminology used in Sufi doctrine, but overall, this poem is far from the abstract and dry scholasticism of Sanai and similar Sufi theoreticians.[15] The task that Nizami set himself had little in common with Sanai's main objectives and thus give his creation particularly distinctive features. Moreover, Nizami's poems can only be labelled Sufi with considerable caveats.

In the preceding section I tried to give a brief account of the activities of the Akhi sect, to which Nizami was affiliated, I am convinced that this sect could more accurately be described as a brotherhood, and that the 'ethereal ectsasies' of the dervishes were alien to it. It placed its objectives very concretely back on earth to improve the daily life of urban and peasant populations.

Following the teaching of his mentor, Nizami dressed his observations in Sufi poetic forms. Religious norms, apparently, were placed at the front. But one only needs to look past this first layer to reach the heart of the poem and begin to understand that its main purpose was to serve rulers in the task of governance: reorganising the present earthly life, or bringing happiness and prosperity to the country. Herein his religious position was his strength, as at that time it could not have been otherwise, yet the poems were already interpreted, not in the interest of the rulers, but rather as rules that would protect people's rights and freedoms.

Every chapter of these poems contains an introduction, a sort of theoretical section, which is followed by a short narrative, illustrating the theoretical position of the chapter. It is striking to notice the courage with which Nizami discusses the monstrosities of his time. Angry protests fill his verses, resonant with the voice of the people of the city, who were already claiming their rights and asking for power.

It seems that the key to understanding all these poems is to be found in the following short narrative (chapter 14):

There was a king who oppressed his subjects / In his pretence he had become like Ḥajjāj

Anything born before morning, in the night, / Would hang on his door by dawn

One better versed in revealing secrets than the sun or moon / Went before the ruler in the morning

He had copied the moon's shadow play / And could cast light on matters like the dawn

He said: 'An old man secretly / Described you as a murderer of innocents, tyrannical and bloodthirsty'

The king was angered by this speech / Saying 'I should have him murdered this very minute'

He ordered the executioner's mat to be spread and sprinkled with sand / Demons fled from his demonic behaviour

A youth hurried to the old man arrow-fast, saying / 'The king has pinned a crime on you!'

The old man abluted and took up his grave shroud / He went before the king and composed his speech

The quick-witted king rubbed his hands / And maliciously searched for a pretext

Saying: 'I hear you have talked about me / Calling me malicious and a murderer of innocents

You know of my kingdom, like Solomon's / Why then do you call me a violent demon?'

The old man said to him, 'I am not asleep / I said worse things about you than what you claim

Old and young are in danger from your deeds / City and village are afflicted by your tricks

I who enumerate your sins / Hold a mirror to your good and bad actions

See the truth in what I say and take heed / And if things are not so, string me up!

One might get the impression that the old man in the story is Nizami himself.

His first compositionis a mirror presented to Bahramshah. The poet is aware of all the dangers that he is facing. That one should never be truthful to the king is a theme constantly repeated in the East. But his great belief requires from him rigour and he fearlessly brandished his mirror for the cruel reprisal of the potentate.

Here is another narrative, which provides a truthful portrait of peasant life:

One day, when Solomon was at leisure / The wind carried him to a pasture

His country faced into the desert / He set his throne on that green board

He saw an old farmer on that flat plain / A scene that rent his heart

A fistful of grain was not to be found in his house / He had sown it in the earth, the granary of the worms

In every corner he had sown grain / And an ear of corn had sprouted from each grain

When the landowner told him of that grain / Solomon disclosed the language of the birds

The young man said 'Go, old man / You had this much, and ought to have eaten it

You're not a sparrow, do not scatter grain / Do not attempt the language of the birds with one like me

You have no spade, do not scratch the desert clay / Deceitful landowner, you won't find any water.

I sowed in black earth / See what I have reaped from what I sowed'

The old man said, 'Do not be offended by my reply / I am beyond cultivating earth and water

I have no care for wet and dry / The grain is mine and the nurture God's

This is my water, the sweat of my back / This is my spade, the tip of my finger

I have no worry of the kingdom or the state / While I live this grain suffices me'

Again we see here a majestic image, truly uncommon for this period, of the beggar-farmer who works without tools in the empty steppes hoping for the spring rains, the powerful force of nature, but help comes from nowhere.

Of course, not all the narratives of this poem contain characters with such anger against the ruling classes, but political advice is scattered throughout all of the verses, most probably on purpose, for in combination they would have induced a strong impression on readers of the feudal system.

In the introduction:

A house is owned by a tyrant / Permanent good fortune comes through clemency

A kingdom lasts because of justice / Your actions gain balance through justice

For how long must you kick up the dust of violence / Spilling your own water and the blood of others?

Since they take gold coins by force of iron / Most kings are blacksmiths

If the keeper of this path is a plunderer / Poverty is better than comfort?

The Shah was this severe censor, shedding innocent blood, depriving people of the fruits of their honest labour, like a highwayman extorting gold by the sword.

This stands in contrast to the great figure of the worker, who is the actual bearer of the honour of humanity, the creator of human happiness. The purpose of life-work:

we came here for the sake of work / Not for the sake of empty conversations[1]

Work does not always bring success, more often than not it is rewarded by "bread for your stomach and a sip of water", but even so, it is not acceptable to grovel for wealth:

I will not suffer injustice from anyone for the sake of riches / But I suffer injustice at the hand of toil

Thus, the fundamental idea in Nizami's first poem is to seek to identify injustice in human society and find ways to address it. These thoughts, as we shall see, occupied the poet's mind all his life. The observations presented already gathered together and by the end of his life they provided an incredible depiction of a brotherly state of freedom where all members of the society work on an equal footing. This picture appears clearly in his last poem, the *Iskandar-nama*, which concluded the last days of his life.

Despite extensive technical skill deployed in this first poem, in which each verse is a unit in itself, it does not contain broader imagery. The theme itself prevents any such picture to be expressed. Yet the great human consciousness, so characteristic of Nizami, already appears here with full strength. With one or two verses, the poet succeeds in revealing the depth of the human soul, to present us the human being with an almost tangible clarity. For instance, in the abovementioned scene, the old man stands in front of the tyrant, who burns with hatred, but cannot look at him in the eyes, and merely rubs his hands with rage. This level of detail is only perceptible through the pen of a great master.

The language in Nizami's first poem is particularly difficult. The poet clearly wanted to demonstrate his proficiency in mastering difficult poetic techniques, and each verse contains refined comparisons, metaphors and other difficult stylistic figures.

Nizami evidently set up this task for himself, as described in the following verses:

> *If I had not done justice to it in speech / I could not have sent it from city to city*

Its complexities were noticed very early on, for two commentaries have come down to us from the end of the thirteenth and the beginning of the fourteenth centuries, containing a great quantity of precious materials, and which assist in analysing the most difficult of verses.

Notes

1. We have not traced this verse in Nizami's work and so have translated it from Berthels' Russian.

Work: Khusraw and Shirin

Nizami's second poem transports us into a completely different set of ideas. The narrative here does not illustrate theoretical positions anymore; it constitutes the fundamental core of the composition.

The topic of the poem existed long before Nizami and was to a certain extent extracted from chronicles of the Sasanian dynasty. Yet parallel to the written tradition, there was naturally an oral one, which in the popular mind was linked to the building of ancient Iranian palaces, known as Qasr-e Shirin and Bisotun. The legends attached to these places in the first half of the tenth century are narrated by the Arab geographer al-Yaqut (d. 1229). The famous historian al-Tabari (d. 921) also reported that many stories were circulating about the Sasanian king, Khusraw Parviz. In Firdawsi's, *Shah-nama*, the section on Khusraw details his intent to "update the book of the ancients".

The story of Khusraw was obviously well-known at the time of Firdawsi, for the poet found it possible to mention it just briefly, relating only the story of Khusraw as ruler, without describing his relationship to Shirin, thus leaving all the beauty of this narrative to Nizami.

If Nizami was not relying on written sources that are simply unknown to us (an idea that is hard to accept for several reasons) then it can be assumed that most of the material was passed on to him orally, which was probably the most usual mode of transmission in Azerbaijan at that time.

It is important to notice that even the basic appearance of the poem itself already informs us about Nizami's decision to move away from the model of Firdawsi. Already by the tenth century, feudal poetry had successfully determined basic principles for different genres of epic poetry. Hence, heroic poems had to include a name in their title along with the word *nama*, meaning 'book', as used by Nizami in the title of his last poem, *Iskandar-nama*. Romantic poems, in which the love relationship stands in the forefront, are an exception to this rule as they introduce the names of the two principal characters together in their title. It is worth mentioning here that the same rules were applied in ancient Greek literature, and this is very unlikely to be coincidental.

Furthermore, heroic poems used a metre called *mutaqarib*, according to the following scheme:

$$\cup -- \mid \cup -- \mid \cup -- \mid \cup -$$

Romantic poetry, already in the eleventh century, tended to make a transition to the so-called *hazaj*:

$$\cup --- \mid \cup --- \mid \cup ---$$

Nizami's poem, written in *hazaj*, contains two names in the title, thereby making it clear that the history of Khusraw's dynasty is not central to it.

I will attempt here to give a brief overview of the course of action of the poem.

The Sasanian king Hurmuz had a son, Khusraw, who became, as he grew up, one of the most handsome young men in Persia. His father loved him passionately, but he watched his behaviour so that when his son carelessly took liberties regarding his relationship to the peasants, he did not hesitate to enact severe punishment.

In Khusraw's entourage, there was a skilful artist, Shapur who had learnt his art in China in the school of the famous Mani. He wandered around the world for a long time and narrated his pilgrimages. One day he told Khusraw that in the mountains by the Caspian Sea, a very powerful queen ruled the land. Her name was Shamira, also known as Mahin Banu (the great lady). Her niece, Shirin, was the most beautiful woman in the world. Having heard this story, Khusraw was longing for Shirin. He decided that he could not live without her and he sent Shapur to Armenia, commanding him to bring this beautiful princess to him.

The task was not simple, and Shapur decided to approach it with the help of his art.

Upon his arrival in Armenia, he stayed in a monastery, whereupon the monks informed him where Shirin and her friends were to be found. He went to the place where they were taking a walk and threw to Shirin a portrait of Khusraw, drawn in the finest possible style, with his best brush. When noticing that the unexpected portrait he threw to Shirin piqued her interest, he came out of his hiding place, approached Shirin and told her about Khusraw and his passionate love. Shapur's story sparked her imagination, and encouraged by Shapur, she ran away from Armenia on the famous horse called Shabdiz which could run faster than any other horse on earth. On her way, she found a stream and tired by heat and thirst, she decided to take a bath.

At the same time, in the Sasanian capital, the machinations of Khusraw's enemies against him and his father become so threatening that the young prince was forced to flee to avoid their wrath. It happened that he came to the a pool in the same stream at the very moment when Shirin was getting into the water. Her face was hidden by her unruly hair, and Khusraw did not recognise her. Captivated by the beauty of the young prince, whom she also did not recognise, she wondered at the way her heart, full as it was with Khusraw, could nevertheless be moved by another.

This scene has always attracted artists' attention and in almost all the illuminated manuscripts of the poem, it is represented in a miniature, which focuses on this particular moment.

The young people left each other. Upon her arrival at Mada'in, Shirin was told that Khusraw was not there. The slaves who had been freed by the prince thought that it was a new female friend and helped her settle into the palace. She did not disclose her identity to them, worked with them and took part in their games.

Khusraw went to Armenia and Mahin Banu, although she was upset about the disappearance of her niece, invited him to spend the winter in the city of Barda'a. At the same time, Shirin was languishing in Mada'in. She remembered that she had met a young man on the way and thought that he must be Khusraw. But the constantly hot climate of the Sasanian capital started to affect her health. She asked for a castle to be built for her somewhere in the mountains, which she was accustomed to from childhood.

The slaves, who were jealous of her because of Khusraw, paid an architect and made sure that the palace would be built in a gloomy place, far from all people.

Finally, Khusraw heard about Shirin and where she was. He explained to Mahin Banu that he would soon bring back her niece and he sent Shapur to Shirin. But at this moment, Khusraw's father, Hurmuz died. A difficult episode then began. The young prince quickly had to return to the capital in order not to lose his father's throne. Shirin went to Barda'a, but again she could not find Khusraw and she went back to her aunt who was delighted.

Khusraw was not successful. The nobles already disliked him and one of them, Bahram Chubin prepared a rebellion and forced Khusraw to save himself in exile. He went naturally to Barda'a, where the two lovers finally met.

If Nizami had wanted to write a typical chivalric novel he would have ended it here. But all of these complicated adventures served to portray the authentic dramatic conflict taking place, not in the superficial course of events, but in the very soul of his hero.

Noticing how Shirin was consumed by her love, Mahin Banu warned her against Khusraw, the great king, who was always surrounded by slaves and used to consider women as toys to satisfy his own passions. She allowed Shirin to spend time with him, but she required from her that she remained chaste. She could become his wife, providing he would marry her officially.

Khusraw, tormented by his passion, chased Shirin and tried to obtain a kiss from her. Yet, in answer to all his pleas, she replied by reminding him that it was inappropriate for a knight to enjoy himself while others had stolen his throne. She concluded by saying that he would have a wife, when he was be able to retrieve his ancestors' heritage.

These words inspired pride in Khusraw and brought him to his senses. He felt that Shirin was right and he was overwhelmed by self-consciousness of his own weakness. The offense that Shirin had inflicted on him pushed him to gather all his strength and start taking action. As he no longer had an army, he sought help from the Byzantine emperor. He received the help he requested, but with it came the hand of the emperor's beautiful daughter, Maryam. Upon his return to Persia from the Byzantine war, he banished Bahram and recovered his father's throne.

But the memory of Shirin would not leave his mind. He had a bad relationship with his young wife. She took power over all his possessions and had the people on her side. Shirin did not forget her beloved one either, but she concealed it thoroughly. Then Mahin Banu died, and the throne was bestowed on Shirin who decided to use this advantage to gain freedom. Giving her governance of the country to a vizier, she went with a large retinue to the castle in the mountains, which had been built for her.

Rumours about her reached Khusraw who aspired to see her, but feared Maryam. Nevertheless, he decided to ask his wife for permission to invite Shirin to Mada'in, providing she would be submissive towards Maryam. The Greek queen entered in a fury and swore that if Khusraw pursued his plan, she would hang herself and Khusraw would have to bring the news to her father.

Then Khusraw sent Shapur to try to convince Shirin to meet him secretly in the palace. As one would have expected, Shirin proudly replied that she would come to the palace as Khusraw's wife only. She could never grovel.

Life in her remote castle started to torment the isolated Shirin. She needed milk, but there was no pasture near the castle and cattle could not be nourished anywhere around, yet Shirin did not want to impose on her servants to bring it to this distant mountain. Here we reach the poem's most dramatic point. Shapur offered that his companion Farhad, a skilful stonecutter, might dig a canal in the rock, through which milk could flow directly from the pasture to the castle. Farhad was summoned but Shirin did not meet him; she talked to him from behind a curtain. But he was so captivated by her bewitching voice that he promised to finish this difficult task in a month. Despite all the hurdles before him, Farhad accomplished the task. Shirin rewarded him, but he was so possessed by his love for her, that, forgetting the reward, he fled to the steppe to hide his distress from strangers.

Rumours about his love reached Khusraw. He was seized by jealousy and decided to call the stonecutter and to forbid him even to dream of this. The meeting between Khusraw and Farhad, presented as a dispute, is one of the most brilliant parts of the poem. With concise and pertinent replies, the two opponents struck each other as if they were fighting with swords. Khusraw noticed that overcoming his adversary or buying his submission with gold was impossible. Hence he determined to assign him an impossible task. He was to carve a road through the mountain, cutting it in two. If he were successful, Khusraw would renounce Shirin.

Farhad started the work and his love gave him a giant's strength to break the stones with his pick. Having heard about his task, Shirin came to see him. Having talked with the stonecutter, she turned back, but her horse slipped on a stone and fell. Farhad took the horse with the queen on his shoulders and carried Shirin back to her castle.

Khusraw that Farhad could accomplish seemingly impossible tasks. He did not dare to withdraw his oath, and so he decided to get rid of him with a trick. A mountaineer was sent to Farhad to announce to him Shirin's alleged death, at which he himself died.

Shirin built a tomb for him and Khusraw was embarassed by the consciousness of his ignoble action. At this time, Maryam died. Thus Khusraw was free, with no more obstacles in front of him, but again he was overwhelmed by doubt. Shirin sent him a letter, in which she comforted him mockingly for his loss. But she added, knowing his flippancy, that he would most probably not cry long over his wife.

It seems that this affected the weak Khusraw. Yet he heard from a beautiful woman from Isfahan named Shikar. He went there and brought her back to Mada'in, which clearly worsened his relationship with Shirin.

During a hunt, Khusraw found himself in the lands of Shirin's castle. Gathering all his strength, he went to her, but Shirin did not welcome him and talked to him from the castle walls. She reproached him for daring to come before her drunk, when he should have sent a noble man to convey her the capital with honour. Khusraw left in despair.

Shirin's strength however gave out. After having expelled him, she ran after him. She arrived secretly in his pavilion, and, taking the place of one of Khusraw's singers, Nekisa, she sang about a gentle gazelle and her longing for her beloved one. After a long duet, she showed herself, and Khusraw threw himself at her feet, but again, she refused him. Only then, Khusraw understood that her chastity was her strongest defence and, gathering all the nobles, he concluded with her a marriage contract.

The wedding with Shirin seemed to him the most beneficial solution. He understood that one should not live for his own pleasure and he tried to learn the art of good governance. But a new cloud overshadowed him. Khusraw and Maryam had had a son, Shiruya, who also admired Shirin's beauty. Supported by the nobles, he seized the throne and sent his father to prison. However, as Shirin joined her husband in the dungeon, Khusraw lost everything but her.

Shiruya decided to finally get rid of him. At night, he paid an assassin with gold to kill the king. Khusraw felt death coming, but as Shirin was deeply asleep, and he did not want to worry her, he preferred to die in silence.

Then Shiruya demanded the victor's spoils. Shirin deceived the murderer. She agreed to all of the terms, but demanded that Shiruya would destroy first everything that could remind her of Khusraw, burn his castle, kill his horse, and that the king himself would organise a sumptuous funeral. Khusraw's body was carried to a crypt. Shirin went to him and, closing the door behind her, she killed herself on the body of her beloved husband. The poem ends with reflections on the world's frailty and the inaccessibility of earthly happiness.

In *Khusraw and Shirin*, Nizami successfully applied the techniques he had already started to use in *Makhzan*. The language shines like gems. Yet, if in the first poem, one feels that Nizami dedicated a lot of attention to this aspect, then in this poem, the language has reached a greater maturity. The technique is not the objective anymore, as it was in *Makhzan*, it is simply a tool in the hands of an unrivalled virtuoso. It reaches its full strength in the descriptions woven into the fabric of the poem and elaborated by the poet into glorious decorations sewn through with all the classical traditions of rhetoric.

But description was not Nizami's purpose when he composed the poem. His main goal was to show the reader the personality of his two heroes. His knowledge of psychology reaches here its peak. The heroes are depicted in all their complexity and contradictions with utmost clarity. Herewith, at the heart of the poem, the real hero is undoubtedly not Khusraw, but Shirin.

All of Nizami's love is given to her. And this is not surprising, when we remember that this marvellous figure was created by Nizami in memory of his most beloved Afaq, whose loss he suffered until his own death. This approach might seem to us natural and understandable, nevertheless, one must bear in mind that for a Muslim audience, it was incredibly bold. Women at that time were toys; merchandise that could be traded with money. This is exemplified in the poem with Khusraw's initial attitude towards them. But the great poet thoroughly insists on their right to be respected, their human quality, their heroism and their courage.

The whole poem is full of stanzas highlighting Shirin's love for people, her care for them and for avoiding burdening them. She is the perfect opposite to Khusraw, for whom the people are simply means to reach his own pleasure and enrichment. He is unable to act; he is, with all his handsomeness and talents, the product of degeneration. In the entire poem, there is only one occasion when it seems that he is acting on his own, and it is precisely when he chooses a despicable way to deal with Farhad. He loves Shirin undoubtedly, but this love is greedy and selfish; a love which does not know how to make any sacrifices in the name of love.

Shirin seems thus to be giving her heart to an unworthy person. The reader is sometimes overwhelmed by resentment towards the idea that Shirin suffers for the sake of this frivolous man, deprived of any dignity. Notwithstanding the question of faithfulness in the story, Nizami points out here a complex issue regarding love, which is presented in very precise and realistic terms. In fact, such women are often victims of their own destiny when they fall in love with someone, stop seeing him, and start loving, not him, but a beautiful representation constructed by their own imagination.

There is also the relationship between Shirin and Farhad. The cruelty towards the unsuccessful lover is somehow unfairly a reproach to her. She knew that he loved her, she witnessed that he fell victim to her, but she could not possibly help him. In her heart, there is no space for any other love. Her love is stronger than herself. She sincerely mourned Farhad and she truly regretted the loss of him, yet she could not overcome her own self. If she had not returned to Khusraw, and had rushed into Farhad's arms, she might have been far happier, but she remained the proud and pure Shirin, preserving the one single love of her life.

To create the character of Shirin, Nizami characteristically left the confines of the Muslim world, and turned his gaze on the Christian Caucasus. There is little doubt that the figure of Shirin like that of her aunt, the queen Shamira, are based in the knowledge that Nizami had about the Georgian Tamara. And although the name 'Shamira', reflects the village of Semiramis, it is not by chance that it resonates with Tamara.

The third major figure of the poem, Farhad, has particular significance. Even though, as mentioned in the summary above, his role is episodic and short because of his dramatic death, it is nonetheless absolutely crucial to the story. He is the perfect opposite of Khusraw, a man who feels a genuine love, does not expect anything for himself, and gives everything, including his life. This love is the love of a hero, which Nizami considers as the true love that has the potential to inspire humanity towards progress.

In other words, by contrasting Farhad with Khusraw, Nizami clearly takes position in favour of the former, and criticises the latter. But Farhad does not belong to the aristocracy. He personifies the city, the artistic craftsman, who studied under the same master as Shapur. With which characteristics does the poet depict him? He is a great hero, with an incredible strength, a talented artist, incontestably honest and noble. It might be that this superhuman strength highlights the fact that he is not a simple being, but rather the people's hero, who is vanquished only by the power of love.

123

Nizami confronts thus two classes through these two figures, and although he allows the representative of the oppressed class to die so as to illustrate that which usually happened at his time, he nevertheless shows as well that this death can only be considered as treachery and betrayal by the ruler. It is as if Nizami wanted to say that in his honest fight against ruler the hero may fall, but he will return sooner or later to demand his rights, and moreover obtain them. In this proud self-affirmation resonates the growing strength of the city and the rise of urban life, which, as has been mentioned above, were disrupted by the violent Mongol invasion.

Nizami's second poem is therefore an outstanding creation, which has no equal in the world of literature. For the first time in the literature of the Near East, human values were presented to readers in all their details and complexity, showing the use of a subject within established traditions, which at the same time bound the poet. Only a genius could overcome these obstacles and utilise the material with such a perfect proficiency.

The people valued Nizami's prodigious creation. After him, his heroes were tightly linked with Azerbaijan and it is not surprising to find a fourteenth-century Azerbaijani poet, Arifi reworking his themes and affirming that the court of one of Farhad's sons (who, it is true, he made made the son of a Chinese empress) was located in Baku, and there also was to be found the cemetery where all of Farhad's family was buried.

Work: Layla and Majnun

Aspects of the history of this poem have already been mentioned, insofar as Nizami wrote it against his own inclination, at the command of the Shirvanshah.

What material did Nizami base this new work on? The hero of this poem, Qays b. Mulawwa, known as Majnun ('possessed by djinns', 'mad'), is thought to be a historical figure according to many Arab critics; a poet, whose verses were preserved after his death around 689.

However, one might argue that Majnun was not a historical figure at all. Ibn al-Kalbi said that the verses about Majnun and the story of his unhappy love for Layla were created by a member of the Umayyad dynasty, who wanted to conceal his identity, which seems to me a very plausible explanation. The author of the verses did not, of course, turn the fables of Majnun into a romance. He published only verses, and a whole series of episodes which would have explained the history of the work's creation, were transmitted, in all probability, solely through oral traditions.

Later on, these fables were gathered and systematically preserved by Arab scholars in several variants. It is possible to determine two main sources. The *Book on Poetry and Poets* by Ibn Qutayba (d. 831) and the *Book of Songs* by Abu al-Faraj al-Isfahani (d. 967). These materials along with some additions, the origin of which is unknown, made their way into the commentary of Abu Bakr al-Walibi, who published Majnun's *diwan* in a version that has come down to us.

All these sources might have been available to Nizami, but we may conclude on the basis of a number of lines that he made the most extensive use of the last and most comprehensive of them. Comparing Nizami's poem with these texts reveals that the poet undertook his task with keen attention and, when necessary for his narrative, he exactly reproduced elements from these sources In other words, Nizami was in a sense even less free than for his previous poem, and it is likely that this was one of the reasons why he was reluctant embark on this task.

The title, like for the previous poem, contains two names, which clearly indicates that the poem's centre of gravity lies in the relationship between the two heroes, i.e. it is not the biography of Majnun, but the story of his love. Yet as we have seen previously, this love assumes a completely different character. The heroic element here is secondary and non-essential. In the foreground are feelings, and therefore the poem can reasonably be described as sentimental and romantic. Nizami's artistic flair allowed him to reflect this in the external form of the poem by using a different variant of the *hazaj* metre with a more intricate rhythm following the following pattern:

$$--\cup\cup\,|-\cup-\cup\,|--$$

The scheme itself clearly shows that the smoothness and breadth of *Khusraw and Shirin*'s metre is not repeated here; the metre contains a characteristic break that gives to the verses a particular nervy and fervent quality.

The plot of the poem is constructed as follows: after a few introductory chapters, among which the chapter containing practical advice to Nizami's son is of particular interest. Nizami comes to the narrative itself. Having no son and heir, the chief of the Bani Amir tribe prayed to God to grant him a successor and after many years, he finally was finally given a son named Qays. When the boy was ten years old, the father sent him to school, where he studied alongside other children and met the young Layla. The children saw each other every day and eventually fell in love with each other. Although they tried to hide their feelings, their secret became known, and passion and fervour were such that he gained the nickname 'Majnun'.

The children were eventually separated from each other, but the separation did not weaken Majnun's feelings – on the contrary, it strengthened them. He could not stand to stay at home and he wandered in the mountains of Najd every day, bewailing his youthful sorrow. His father, who begrudged nothing for the sake of his beloved son, decided to assist him and went with opulent company and rich presents to ask for Layla's hand. Her father however did not approve of the match and replied:

> *He shows signs of madness / A madman cannot be our mate*
>
> *You know how the Arabs find fault / What would they say if I did this?*

Although the separation was already difficult for Majnun, this misfortune further wounded his heart. He again ran away to the mountains, driven so seriously mad that his family were deeply worried about him. It was decided that he should be sent to Mecca to pray at the Ka'ba. It is worth noticing here that in his serious poems Nizami did not usually include miraculous elements. I am inclined to believe that Nizami introduced this journey not because he believed in the miracle of the Ka'ba, but merely from the idea that a change of scene on a journey can weaken the feeling of love. Travel as an escape from unhappy love in ancient literature, for example in *Ring of the Dove* the by the famous Arab author Ibn Hazm.

When arrived in, his father commanded him to put his hands on the ring of the Ka'ba's door and to ask for deliverance from his yearning. He spoke to him at length and concluded with these words:

Help me, I am afflicted by passion / Release me from the affliction of passion

But these were precisely the words that he should not have spoken. As soon as Majnun heard the word 'love', his passion reached a new intensity. Grabbing the Ka'ba's ring he exclaimed:

My nature is fed on passion / May I have no fate but passion!

Thereupon, he left his homeland and wandered around sticking close to Layla's nomadic people. At this stage, the reader understands that his only cure would be union with his beloved. Layla's relatives, when they learned he was roaming around in the vicinity, were filled with rage and the girl's father swore that he would kill him if he saw him. When Majnun's father heard this, he sought out his son and warned him, but threats and exhortations were useless and Majnun continued to wander in the mountains of Najd. At the same time, a wealthy man, Ibn Salam beseeched Leyla's father to consent to his marrying the girl, arguing that this would end the matter entirely, but her father asked merely to give some the girl some time to calm herself.

During his wanderings, Majnun met the powerful chief Nawfal, and having heard about his misfortunes, Nawfal, resolved to settle the matter. Again, it seemed that hope was smiling but Layla's father was stubborn. Nawfal took up arms, and went into battle. At first he suffered defeat, but eventually gathering his strength, he inflicted a decisive blow against his enemy. Layla's father turned to his last resort. He declared that he would behead his daughter to prevent Majnun having her. And thus Majnun's last hope disappeared. He abandoned civilisation, wandering in the desert freeing gazelles from traps, because their, eyes reminded him of Layla's and talking with from traps, because the birds and other animals. More and more, he became one with nature and cut himself off from human society.

Nevertheless, he made one final attempt to see Layla and disguised as a beggar he went to her house. But as soon as he saw her, he lost all reason, burst into tears and fled to the mountains. This was the culminating disaster, and there was no going back.

Layla did marry, but when the happy husband tried during their first night to approach her, she slapped him in the face so strongly that she almost killed him. After that, he never attempted again to come close to her and loved her from a distance. At that point, she would hide her yearning no longer.

Majnun's father was so affected by the loss of his son that he became sick. With great difficulty he made his way through the desert and eventually found his son and begged him to spend his last days with him. Majnun was touched by his sorrow, but coming back was impossible. He said:

*Dig a grave and place your hand upon it / Imagine that
a drunken lover has died*

Majnun heard the news and he spent the whole night at
his grave, but in the morning he went back to the desert.
By chance then a passer by delivered a letter from Layla, to
which he replied, delighted.

His uncle Salim took care of him; he brought him food and
clothes in the desert. Then his mother came to him and tried
to convince him to come back, but again unsuccessfully. She
died as well, and Majnun's sorrow increased even further.

Betraying her husband's trust, Layla summoned Majnun
through Salim. But their love was too pure: she could not
bear too enact such a scene and during their liaison she
remained hidden behind dense foliage and only listened to
his passionate songs at a distance. Subsequently Majnun's
fame as a master of love songs travelled around the world.
Coming from Baghdad, the young Salam acquired Majnun's
trust and lived with him for a while to learn all of his songs.

At that time, Layla's husband died from a fever. It seemed
that all obstacles had now disappeared and their union was
thus possible. However it was already late. Truly, Majnun
did not need Layla anymore, as even far away from her,
he was living only for her. Autumn arrived and Layla died,
exhausted by her longing.

When Majnun heard about her death, he rushed to her
grave. He returned several times for hours lying on the
mound over her grave, entrusting her dead body with his

secrets. The wild animals that he befriended in the steppe protected him and were not afraid of his presence. Finally, during one of this visits, death came also to him. It was only possible to bury him after a several years, when the wild animals left; before that, no one could approach his body.

Thus, from a starting point of the random, disconnected episodes provided by his sources, the author moves to a complete picture. He gave himself the task of showing how Majnun's love became an uncurable passion, which could only end in death. With extraordinary proficiency, further episodes are introduced to delay the inevitable conclusions. Thus, at the early stages of the narrative, there is still hope, still the possibility of turning back, but with each step, each augmentation of his despair, his passion becomes stronger and stronger.

An unusual and subtle feature is the death of Ibn Salam, about which Arab sources are silent. It shows that at this stage, Majnun's love is already detached from its object and has reached its apogee, where the poet's fantasies can find satisfaction in his own suffering alone. While Nizami presented in Shirin an active and socially useful love, here we are shown passionate love, which excludes the person from society, and, while it might assist in the creation of immortal of art, their creator. All of this psychological description was only one of the tasks the poet set himself. It should not be forgotten that Nizami wrote every single one of his works with the specific aim of exerting an influence on society and making it better.

It is not by chance that it was precisely here, in the preface of this poem, that he employed the dialogue with his son and his homilies to him. If we compare this introduction with the rest of the poem, we can distinguish three types of fatherly love: a) Majnun's father, who gave way in everything to his son and thereby ruined him; b) Layla's father, who did not take into consideration his daughter's own interest and held honour higher than her happiness; c) Nizami himself, a loving father, who nonetheless observed life soberly and warned his son against the attraction of false ideals.

Recalling, furthermore, that the poem was commissioned by the Shirvanshah, who had a son as well, it becomes clear that Nizami wanted to use this poem to influence ruler, and indicate the right path for his son's education. He rejected the cruel feudal family pattern where unlimited power was placed in the father's hands, and instead defended a family based on mutual trust and love.

In the end, curiously enough and in accordance with the sources, Nizami tries not to damage the romance's literary-historical character in his poem. Majnun is a poet, and Nizami uses this to reveal the way he composed his own lyrics and how they, though composed in the desert, remote from people, have nevertheless been preserved for us.

Hence, in spite of encountering all sorts of difficulties, he completed this task and created a picture of incredible clarity and perfection. The image of Majnun joined the ranks of favourite Near Eastern images, but it broke out of the confines of the written word, crossing into folklore, to acquire everlasting life.

While the story of *Khusraw and Shirin* gave rise to numerous imitations, the versions of *Layla and Majnun* are innumerable. Its themes were particularly appreciated among Sufi poets, who tried to highlight the 'unearthly' aspects of Majnun's love. The fact is that while Nizami's poem allows mystical Sufi interpretations, it has no need of them and remains fully convincing and engaging when understood realistically.

Among the imitations it is worth highlighting, in close connection with Azerbaijan, the great work of the famous Fizuli, one of the rare versions of *Layla and Majnun* which stands besides Nizami's without shame. Fizuli's poem is particularly significant for Azerbaijani literature, for it was written in the author's native language, which made it all the more accessible for readers and hence planted deeper the story of the unfortunate lovers as part of the canon of Azerbaijani folklore.

Work: The Seven Beauties

Having been given the opportunity to choose the theme of his next poem, Nizami turned again to ancient Iranian chronicles. But as he explained, his predecessor, Firdawsi, had already successfully described all of the details and events. Repeating that which was well narrated in the past seemed incorrect to Nizami.

Nonetheless, Nizami in fact chose a character whom Firdawsi had already explored: the figure of the beloved hero from the Sasanian period, the king Bahram Gur. This king, whom the chronicles identify as the son of Yazdegird I, Bahram V (420-438), is one of the most interesting in the Sasanian chronicles. The historical figure appears here under layers of old Near Eastern myth. Thanks to the similarity between his name and the old god Verethragna and clearly with the help of analogical transformations from Georgian and Armenian sources, the Sasanian king was turned into a cosmic hunter, an enlightened hero, who was limitless in his feelings, so that he was as unrestrained in love as he was in hatred.

Nizami stated that he had decided to use the fragments that Firdawsi had ignored, and to build up a story from these crumbs, which could be attributed to old legends. Yet we should consider the fact that this choice was not only intended to overcome Firdawsi's "imperfections". Most likely, Nizami purposefully focused on a hero whose name was Vahagn and Vakhtang, famous in Armenia and Georgia, and having a strong link with old Caucasian legends. In this regard, one shall not forget that in Nizami's eyes, *Khusraw and Shirin* was first of all linked to the Caucasus.

It is still impossible at present to gather all the sources used by Nizami for this poem . This task is still ahead of us.. For now it is only possible to compare the similarities and differences between the poems of Nizami and Firdawsi.

In order to develop the chapters of the *Shah-nama* dedicated to Bahram Gur, Firdawsi, like for all the Sasanian sections of the poem, was limited by the official chronicles available to him, which described the different stages of V's life. Nevertheless, Firdawsi did not limit himself to these chronicles. The introductory chapters, devoted to Bahram's birth, his ascent to the throne, his measures to improve the country, etc., undoubtedly follow the chronicles, but episodes that form the core of the text depict Bahram as a marvellous hunter; a courageous knight who fights with all kinds of fantastic beasts; as a passionate lover, for whom women from all countries and all classes would gather in the palace. Even though these stories might to some extent be reflected in the chronicles, they go back to the depths of antiquity and could have been known to Firdawsi through other channels than official Sasanian reports.

Firdawsi's work is typically at its sharpest and most expressive in these episodes, as for instance during Bahram's clash with his beloved Azade while out hunting, and the story of Bahram and the water-carrier, Lambak, and the charming anecdote of the young shoemaker, and the adventure of Bahram at the mill, etc., each of which illustrates the best poetry of the Sasanian section of the work.

Interestingly, Nizami maintained in his poem this two-fold division of the sources. Like Firdawsi's work, his poem comprises a main narrative line giving the history of the reign of the king, Bahram, and t supplementary sections made up of the stories about him. Nevertheless, in both parts, Nizami willingly distanced himself from the deeply rooted tradition of Firdawsi. Hence, he chiefly used Bahram's story to achieve his goal of highlighting the techniques of government administration, to condemn the wrath of rulers and prevent it. Hence he inserted parts that abandon the traditional cycle of Bahram's legends, introducing folklore tales not linked with Bahram.

As in the two previous poems, the question of love is central, in Bahram's life as well as - and especially - in the remaining parts of the story. Yet love is this time not tied to any heroic or tragic development. Among the range of forms that it adopts, it mostly remains a happy theme and Nizami strives thoroughly to highlight positive moments. In keeping with the changing, fantastical character of the theme itself, Nizami modified the rhythm again and chose this time the whimsical and capricious *khafif*:

$$- \cup - \, | \, - \cup - \cup \, | \, - \cup \cup -$$

The basic shape of the poem is as follows.

It begins with the usual introductory chapter, after which the poet turns to his patron Kurpa Arslan. Praising him, he tries to establish a comparison between him and the hero of his poem, pointing out that the sultan "pierced the front and back legs of a ravenous wolf with a forked arrow". Along with the sultan, there is reference to his wife and two of his sons, Nusrat al-Din Muhammad Shah and Falak al-Din Ahmad. Commenting on Kurpa Arslan's values, the poet said that he is not like other Shahs, saying:

> *They stage a feast when they drink blood / And give bread when they take souls*

According to Nizami, Arslan did not let the ploys of alchemists trick him, and refused to believe blindly in charlatans. Following praise for Allah, like in the other poems, come the verses:

> *The only testament to men is speech / All else is empty*

One can conclude from remarks mentioned in passing in this chapter that Nizami, at that time, somehow lost the Ildigizid village given to him:

138

I who have loosed a hundred knots / The lord of a village, outside the village

If a guest should arrive from the road / Who will entertain him?

The introduction ends with words of advice to his son, through which we can trace the same constant thread of Nizami's thought that we have observed already:

I who am satisfied on my own grain / Am content like an oyster in its shell

It is better that contentment be my companion / What is a life of service to me?

It is better to treat others to bread from one's own cloth / Than to eat halva at a base man's feast

From this point the poet carries on with the main narrative. Bahram was the son of the vile Yazdagird (399-420), who was called the "sinner", because of his dislike for warfare, which won him hatred from the noble warlords, while his unwillingness to comply with the increasing number of claims laid by the Zoroastrian clergy alienated him from the principal representatives of the intelligentsia, the Mobeds (Zoroastrian priests).

Because of the difficult situation which prevailed in the country, Bahram's father sent him to be educated by the ruler of Yemen, Nu'man. After four years in the hot Yemeni climate, the prince's health was deteriorating and it was decided that a castle should be built in the mountain, where Bahram would enjoy more fresh air.

Simnar,[17] a builder, was found, who was a skilful architect building many monuments in Egypt and Syria. Simnar started his work, and after five years the stupendous castle of Khavarnak stood there, possessing a miraculous property which made it change its colour three times a day, from blue to white and then yellow.

Simnar received a generous reward. While showing his gratitude for the gift, he inadvertently mentioned that he could have built an even greater palace with seven colours. Fearing that the architect would build such a palace for someone other than the king and that it would eclipse this one, Nu'man ordered him thrown from the castle tower. Thus Simnar, instead of the reward for his labour, found only death.

The palace offered the most refined delights. It was praised and poems were written about it, but Nu'man fretted about the crime he had committed and he wandered in the desert to redeem his sin. His son Munzir was in charge of Bahram's education, including the Arabic, Persian and Greek languages, but also a whole range of sciences, including astrology, and of course, the mastery of weapons.

Bahram's favourite activity was hunting wild asses (*gur*). He would kill among them only the adults older than four years and the young ones he would mark them with his sign and leave them in the desert. His strength was such that he once pierced with one arrow a lion and an ass on which it had pounced, after which his arrow still pierced the ground. This achievement is pictured in the paintings of Khavarnak.

Once, while hunting, Bahram chased an ass until sunset, eventually reaching a cave where a dragon was sleeping. It appeared as though the ass led him there to take revenge for the killing of its offspring. Bahram killed the dragon and intended to leave with its head, but the ass entered the cave and seemed to call him and following it, he found an immense hoard of treasure. In order to carry it all, three hundred camels were needed, and Bahram presently distributed all this wealth to his friends. His fight with the dragon was also depicted on Khavarnak's walls.

Wandering in his castle, Bahram discovered a room that he had never seen before. On the wall of this room, there were seven portraits of beautiful ladies, in the middle of whom he was himself standing in his king's apparel. This was a forecast of his future. The young prince was extremely pleased and he ordered the room to be locked forbidding anyone to enter. He would himself go only when he was drunk to dream about his fortunate future.

At this time, Yazdegird died. The nobles fought to take the throne from Bahram, pretending that the prince would be as much of an enemy to them as his father. An old relative was instead chosen and the throne was given to him. This news reached Bahram and full of anger, he went to Iran with the help of Munzir. Nizami introduced here a small digression to explain that this has all aleady been narrated

It is not my duty to repeat what has been said

Two craftsmen renewed old coin / With the alchemy of speech

One made true silver from copper / And now the other has turned silver into pure gold

In other words, Nizami praised his version of the story higher than the *Shah-nama*.

At the frontier of Iran, Bahram received a letter from the new Shah asking for forgiveness. He sat on the throne not out of his own will, but only as the caretaker of the country, not the Shah. He envied Bahram and his ignorance of the worries that trouble a king. He acknowledged that Bahram was the legal successor, but as the aristocracy still rejected him because of his father's legacy it would be better for him to renounce the throne.

Bahram was full of anger, yet he restrained himself and replied that, "the throne "belonged to my father. If he was a sinner, the blame cannot fall on me". At the end of the letter, he decided to show mercy and justice. On receiving the missive, the Mobeds agreed that he was right. However, they found another pretext: they had taken an oath to whoever was on the throne, and they would not break that oath without good reason. Bahram replied: "there is no need to break it, I will "gently" take the crown from him myself".

The dragon has reached the cave entrance / Should it ask the spider's permission to enter?

Whoever takes the crown from between two lions / The people will consider him crowned that day

Hearing this reply, the old man was scared and wanted to renounce the throne. But the Mobeds insisted that Bahram should be left to carry out his proposal, and if he did not dare to do it, then the old man could keep his throne. The lions were prepared. Without the slightest fear, Bahram went up to them, killed both beasts of prey, and seized his father's crown. Thereafter no obstacles remained and he came to the throne. On the day of his coronation he addressed the people in a long speech, promising mercy and justice. And in reality the country started again to flourish. Seeing that everything was back in order, Bahram paid little attention to government and instead focused incessantly on amorous adventures.

The country thrived so much that the inhabitants grew proud and became cruel and unjust. They were convinced that their wealth would last forever. Then the country was punished through poor harvests and terrible famine. Bahram ordered all the state granaries to be opened. Wealthy people bought the crops and distributed them to the needy, and that which remained was left for the birds. Thus life went on for four years and only one person died of hunger at that time, a death for which Bahram cried bitterly feeling that he was responsible. The well-being of the people increased again, the population grew, and the country became so strong that it did not even think of creating an army. Bahram, who intended to make life more joyful, gathered the best musicians from all over the country and distributed them across the cities.

Here Nizami introduced a reminder of the former narrative about Bahram's encounter with his beloved slave, which was brilliantly presented by Firdawsi, but where the difference in his interpretation is the most apparent.

Bahram was hunting and his beloved slave-girl, Fitne (Azade in Firdawsi's poem) has accompanied him. While he was boasting about his talent in archery, the slave-girl suggested to him a difficult task: shooting a gazelle in the head through its hoof. Bahram succeeded, but his slave, instead of showing admiration, told him calmly that this was nothing extraordinary; it was just a matter of practice. Furious, Bahram wanted to kill her, but, because he was unwilling to spill a woman's blood, he ordered an officer to kill her. The slave convinced the officer to defer the sentence and asked him persistently to tell Bahram that his order had been carried out. If the Shah was pleased, nothing would have to be done, but if he killed her and the Shah regretted his decision, she would be saved. After a week officer informed Bahram about the death of his slave and the Shah cried bitterly, for he loved her truly. Then the officer took her away to the countryside and lodged her in his castle. The castle was built on a mountain, and its *iwan* was accessed by way of a large and high staircase built of stone. On the arrival of Fitna in the village, a new calf was born and she picked it up and carried it up the stairs. Thus she carried it every day and thanks to this training, she acquired such strength that she was able to carry it up even when it had reached its adult weight.

Fitne seized an opportunity when the Shah was hunting nearby to invite him to the castle. The Shah came, climbed the sixty steps of the stairs and had a feast in the *iwan*. After the wine, he praised the location of the castle, but he asked the master how he thought he would climb the stairs when he reached the age of sixty. The captain replied that it would not be a problem as, surprisingly, he had a girl in the castle who could carry a bull up these stairs. The miracle was shown to Bahram. The Shah was amazed, but he exclaimed:

> *The king said: 'This is not strength / Rather, you have practised from the beginning'*

To this was replied:

> *She said, 'The king owes a great debt that must be paid / Practice for a cow, but not for an onager?'*

Bahram recognised his dear Fitne. He compensated her master and married her. At this time, a new danger threatened Bahram. The Chinese Khaqan heard that Bahram was busy with drinking and love, so he decided to conquer Iran. He crossed Central Asia with three hundred thousand archers and reached Transoxiana. Bahram's army, after such a long idle period, was not ready to fight and Bahram fled. When he heard the news, the Khaqan rejoiced, and started celebrating and feasting. Bahram gathered three hundred soldiers and attacked the Khaqan's camp in the darkness of the night and thanks to the effect of surprise they secured a resounding victory.

Thereafter, he gathered the nobles and remonstrated with them bitterly: their courage was fake, they were good at nothing. The following words of are of particular interest:

> *'Whom have I seen who stepped forward / And struck the enemy or conquered a country?*
>
> *One tells tall tales that he is descended from Iraj / Another claims to be an Arash in skill*
>
> *One takes his name from Giv and another from Rustam / One's nom-de-guerre is 'tiger' and the other's 'lion'*
>
> *But I have not seen anyone who fought / Or who acted when the time for deeds came*

These verses can be interpreted as the expression of Nizami's disdain towards the native Iranian aristocracy, which boasted of its origins from ancient heroes, but had already degenerated and fallen into a state of near impotence.

Having gained such a victory, Bahram decided it was time to make his dream come true and in various ways, he gathered the seven princesses whose portraits he had seen in Khavarnak. They were Indian, Chinese/Turkestani, Khwarazmian, Slav, Maghrebi, Byzantine and Iranian.[18]

One of Simnar's students offered to build seven palaces for these princesses with domes and different colours for each of them, matching a day of the week and the planet, which is associated to the appropriate day.

Having received the order, the architect finished this immense work in two years. The domes were matching the following scheme:

1. Black, Saturn, Saturday.

2. Yellow, Sun, Sunday.

3. Green, Moon, Monday.

4. Red, Mars, Tuesday.

5. Turquoise, Mercury, Wednesday.

6. Sandal, Jupiter, Thursday.

7. White, Venus, Friday.

This division is extremely interesting, for it matches perfectly the ancient Babylonian astronomical conception on which the calendars of Europe were based. The days of the week in the Muslim world were not named according to the astrological traditions but simply as a chronological list: the first after Saturday, the second after Saturday, etc. The European naming system is based on a much distorted form of the planets' names, and each day is associated with a planet in the actual order given by Nizami. This can be easily observed in a couple of examples (based on Nizami's order): Satur-day is the day of Saturn, Sun-day (in German Sonn-Tag) is the day of the Sun, Mon-day, in French lun-di (from the Latin *lunae dies*) is the day of the Moon, Tuesday, in French mar-di (*martis dies*) is the day of Mars,

Wednesday, in French mercre-di (*mercurii dies*) is the day of Mercury, Thursday, in French jeu-di (*iovis dies*) is the day of Jupiter, Friday, in French vendre-di (*veneris dies*) is the day of Venus. In other words, this precise concordance shows how accurately Nizami preserved this ancient tradition, which had almost fallen out of use in the Muslim world by the twelfth century.

The construction of the palaces came to an end, and so Nizami depicts for us a week in Bahram's life. On Saturday, all dressed in black, Bahram visited the Indian princess in the black palace. After the usual treats, the wine and the music, he asked her to tell him a story. Her narrative is the starting point of the aforementioned series which constitutes undoubtedly the core of the romance. In these narratives, Nizami used the rich folklore to let his creativity express itself freely. Despite his own scepticism towards supernatural narratives, and the lack of any such material in the first three of his poems, which were constructed exclusively on human relationships, here he enters an entirely magical world. Intertwining these narratives with more realistic details, he stepped outside the boundaries of the traditional framework to achieve a flexible brilliance which is so convincing that the reader forgets he is in a fantastic world. Nizami's stories show that in this difficult genre he had no equal. His masterful interpretations are comparable with the greatest creations of the Romantics, such as the E.T.A. Hoffmann's famous tales – especially as their persuasive force is achieved by similar means, through the interweaving of fantastic elements and trivial details of daily life.

One must also consider the fact that Nizami's task was made incredibly difficult by the general plan of the whole romance which is meant to illustrate love, but constantly reaches towards higher levels of enlightenment and purity[19] Secondly, each story had to be linked with the colour of the respective palace as well as the planet. Nevertheless, notwithstanding this apparently difficult task, Nizami succeeded in creating these novellas, which can be counted among his best creations. Their content can be briefly summarised as follows.

1. The Black Pavilion

It is said that in the Indian princess's childhood a venerable woman, always dressed in black, used to visit her house. Regarding the reason behind her dress, she would answer that she was the slave of a king. He was affectionate and tender, and he used to receive many strangers in his house and to debate with them. One day, he disappeared, vanished for a long time and when he came back, he was dressed all in black from head to toe and he would never wear any other colour. One night, she dared to ask him the reason for this and he told her the following story. Among his travel companions, one was dressed in black. The king wanted to know what made him choose such a gloomy colour. He refused to tell him for a long time, but then he narrated that in China there is a beautiful city full of flowers. It is called the 'city of those who are astonished', and all its inhabitants wore black. He did not want to say more and he left. Moved by curiosity, the king decided to investigate this riddle for himself. He went to the city and there became friends with a young man. After having offered to him elaborate presents, he finally asked him to divulge the secret, and the young man was distressed by the question but he could not but oblige. When night came, he led the king to some ruins outside the city and there was a big basket tied with a rope. Seeing no other way out, the king sat in the basket, which went directly into the air, setting him at the top of the highest tower and almost making him die from fear. Soon an immense bird came to the tower and alighted there to sleep. When in the morning it was about to take flight, the king decided to take this opportunity and seizing its leg the bird took him up. After a while, the bird started to descend and the king let go falling into beautiful countryside: a luxurious garden, full of fruit trees bearing tiny lights. Behind him appeared an enchantingly beautiful woman, such beauty as he had never before seen in his life. The princess was aware of his presence and called him to her throne. First, he was offered fruits and wine, but quickly, kisses and embraces followed. She confessed her love to him and promised him happiness under one condition: he had to content himself with kisses only for that day. At night, she offered to bring the favourite of her slaves. The girl who was brought to him led him to a beautiful palace, where he indulged himself in amusements.

In the morning, he woke up alone. He wandered a long while around the garden and at night, everything repeated itself. The flame in his heart grew stronger and stronger, but he maintained his resolve. He spent thus twenty five nights. Finally, on the thirtieth night, the lover started to become more demanding. The beautiful princess asked to delay for one more night but he refused to agree to this. She begged him for indulgence, to close his eyes for a second, while she was changing her clothes, but as he opened his eyes again, the king found himself in the basket, in which he had begun his adventure. After a few moments his young friend, who understood what was going on in the king's soul, said: "You see, you can now only maintain silence and wear mourning clothes". Hence he dressed always in black from this day on, and the narrator inherited this habit from him. The story ends with praise for the colour black.

2. The Yellow Pavilion

The story of the king who sold the slave

A king of Iraq, who had heard from his horoscope that women would bring him poverty, decided not to marry. Instead, he bought beautiful slaves. Yet the beloved girls quickly became spoilt and began behaving arrogantly. The reason for their behaviour was that they received constant flattery from an old maidservant. Thus the king had to keep buying new slaves in the search for his ideal: a modest and humble slave. Once the slave trader brought a new group of slaves. One of them captivated the king with her beauty, but the trader warned him against buying her, saying that the girl was unapproachable and cruel. Ignoring his comment, the king bought her. As a maid, she proved irreplaceable, but she refused to act as a lover. One time, the tormented king was telling her the beautiful story of King Solomon and his beloved Bilqis, and he asked her to tell him the truth and explain to him the reason for her cruelty. The slave narrated that in her family all the women died while giving birth to their first child and she did not want to be like one of these women, so she did not want to be his wife. Knowing her secret, the king started finding ways to attract the beautiful girl and make her forget this danger. Here the old maidservant came to his aid. She advised the king to make her jealous, in which he succeeded. The slave consumed by jealousy confessed her love for him. The king then explained to her his stratagem and they were reconciled. Being passionately in love with her, he covered her with gold and jewellery and the story ends with praise for the colour yellow.

3. The Green Pavilion

In the Sultanate of Rum, there was a man named Bishr. One day, he saw a girl in the street and was captivated by her. However, he did not follow her and decided to endure his pain. To deal with his issue, drank went to Jerusalem and on his way back, he travelled with a companion, the so-called Malikha, who was outwardly very kind, but secretly wicked and cruel. He pretended to possess extended knowledge and explained all the phenomena that happened on their way.

They soon crossed a desert where they suffered from thirst. They finally reached a tree, under which there was, buried in the ground, a great jug full of icy water. Bishr thought that this had been set there by a saintly person as a prayer, but according to Malikha, it was a trap, built by a hunter to catch prey. The two companions tasted the water and drank it. Malikha decided to bathe in the water, even if it might break the jug. Bishr advised him not to do so, but the other insisted. It was in fact a deep well and on jumping into it, Malikha drowned. Bishr pulled him out, buried him, gathered his belongings and went home alone, but from Malikha's pocket fell a purse with a thousand dinars in gold. Bishr decided to give this money to his relatives, so with great difficulty he found Malikha's house, and met his widow. As she heard about her husband's death, she sighed in relief: "he was a wicked person and I am glad to be rid of him". She expressed her will to marry Bishr. She thus removed her veil and Bishr recognised the very woman by whom he had been charmed in the street. As a sign of happiness, Bishr decided to wear only green clothes, like the inhabitants of heaven.

4. The Red Pavilion

In the Russian lands lived a princess as beautiful as the moon. She was skilful in all the sciences and she even learned witchcraft. Her beauty was known around the world and suitors from every country would come to ask for her hand. However, she did not even want to talk with them, and her father decided to build a castle in the mountain with a secret entrance, and safeguarded by statues that would cut in two anyone who tried to enter. Thereafter, she drew her own portrait and wrote under it the conditions under which someone might be eligible to marry her. The brave man had to be able to decode talismans, in order to find the secret entrance, and would have to unravel the riddles that she would set for him. Only then would she consider marrying him and this declaration was placed on the mountain's passes. Many people admired the portrait, many tried their luck, but they all died under the blows of the secret guardians. Their heads were hung on the city's walls, which were soon covered with skulls.

It was finally the turn of a young prince. To ensure he would achieve his goal, he began by going to a famous artist from whom he learned arcane science. Next he put on the red garments of revenge for the injustice inflicted and went forth to achieve his task. Next he succeeded in solving all the obstacles he encountered and all the riddles that were set for him by unfaithful beauty. Captivated by his intelligence and his inventiveness, the princess agreed to marry him, and their wedding was celebrated immediately sparing no expense. In memory of his task, the young man started wearing red clothes only, for red is also the colour of happiness.

5. The Turquoise Pavilion

There was in Egypt a young merchant called Mahan. One day, as he was wandering in the garden with his friends, his business companion came to him and informed him that a caravan was arriving with his goods, promising him great profit. Mahan went to the city gate but the sun had already set and he had to wait until the morning. His friend advised him not to wait, but to try collect the packages by night and he would thus also save the payment of the mandatory tax. Mahan liked the idea and he followed his companion, but then the latter led him to an unknown desert and suddenly disappeared. In the desert, he encountered terrifying creatures, man-eating ghouls, and it was only with great difficulty that he managed to save himself. He finally reached a marvellous garden, plentiful with fruit and fresh water. However, the garden was watched by a guardian, an old man, who was armed with a huge club. Noticing the poor young man, he pitied him and allowed him to stay in the garden, but he set one condition: at night, he would have to climb the tree, sit there and not come down until the morning, regardless of what was happening in the garden.

Mahan climbed the designated tree and wanted to sleep, but in the middle of the night, the garden was suddenly filled with ravishingly beautiful girls. By a pool beside his tree, they set up a banquet, which was presided over by a beauty who sat in the seat of honour.

She noticed Mahan and started calling him to her. At first, Mahan remembered what the old man had said to him and refused, but he then climbed down, sat beside the beautiful lady and took part in the feast. Once his fear disappeared, he embraced the lady and kissed her on her ruby-red lips. All of a sudden, she transformed herself into a dreadful ifrit, an evil spirit with wild boar's tusks. The monster squeezed Mahan in its embrace until morning and mocked him, and Mahan, only half conscious, lay helpless in its arms. When the morning arose, this witchery disappeared and instead of the garden, a vile wasteland appeared, covered with carrion. Only with the help of the mysterious al-Khizr did he manage to get away from this awful place and back to his hometown. As a sign of mourning, he wore only blue clothes from that day onwards.

6. The Sandal Pavilion

Two young men, named Khayr (*good*) and Sharr (*bad*) went out on the road together. They got lost in a desert where they suffered from thirst. Sharr had brought water and Khayr asked to buy just a drop for two precious rubies that belonged to him, but Sharr refused. He feared that once in the city, Khayr would give him other stones than the ones he was expecting. He required him instead to cede his two eyes. The young man's suffering was such that he agreed to this. Sharr blinded him, robbed him, and disappeared. Khayr remained alone:

He rolled in dust and blood / It was better that he had no eyes to see himself

He was then picked up by a wealthy herdsman of Kurdish origins, whose daughter had just had an accident. The Kurd knew of a tree, which could heal his blindness and her disease. Khayr was cured; he married the girl and received as a dowry all of her father's herd.

Soon after that, he took advantage of the miraculous leaves of the tree and cured the Shah's daughter of her epilepsy. He was given her hand and he became king. One day, Sharr was brought to him, as he was accused of some vile crime demanding reprisal. Although he reproached him for his past actions, Khayr released him. His father-in-law, however, could not restrain himself and chased down the villain and cut off his head. The story ends by explaining that the leaves of the healing tree had the colour of Sandalwood.

7. The White Pavilion

A rich young man had in his possession a garden outside the city. One day, he arrived there and heard some music from inside, but the gate was locked and when he knocked noone opened it, so the young man climbed the wall and entered the garden. A whole group of young girls were wandering around in his garden. Thinking he was a thief, they tried to beat him, but calmed themselves when they realised that he was the owner of the garden. Apparently, all the beautiful girls of the town were gathering in the garden to entertain themselves and the young man was advised to choose the one he liked the most for his own pleasure. From the old pavilion, he watched through a chink in the wall the beautiful girls, who were bathing, and pointed at one of them who was was brought to him. They wanted to give themselves over to fun and amusement, but several obstacles prevented them. In the end, the young man lost heart and concluded that destiny itself had saved him from sin and that it was better to follow the correct custom and ask the girl, whom he admired so greatly already, to marry him. The story ends with praises for the colour white, which is the symbol of purity.

In spring the following year, the Khaqan came to Iran again. Bahram wanted to fight him, but he had neither an army nor money. His vizier, Rast-Rawshan, advised him to collect money by force from the population, so Bahram gave him full power and in a short while, the whole country was ruined. Nobody informed Bahram about these events, but an unexpected encounter with an old shepherd revealed these problems to the king and he summoned his vizier to explain himself. The innocent victims who had been imprisoned in the dungeon by the cruel vizier were duly released.

Here again the seven-sided story presents the complaints of the unjustly accused, released by the king from the dungeon. These incredible scenes of despotism and violence are described by Nizami with clarity and spontaneity to show the monstrous bullying by the authorities that the population was forced to bear at that time. This was clearly an act of accusation and condemnation leveled against the feudal society of Nizami's time.

Deeply shocked, Bahram threw his vizier in prison. Thereupon, a messenger from the Khaqan came, which revealed clearly that the vizier had not only ruined the country and raised the defiant population against Bahram, but he had also entered into negotiations with the Khaqan, promising him to open the city's gate for him and to facilitate his victory.

These events affected Bahram considerably. He renounced his previous lifestyle and released his harem. The only entertainment which he could not abandon was hunting, and one day, a wild ass that he shot twice, fled to a cave again, in repetition of what had happened to him when he was young. His servants and his army waited for his return, but Bahram did not return. Suddenly, dust came out of the cave and a terrible voice said "Go home, the Shah is busy!" They entered the cave, but it was not deep and there was no other way out. Bahram's mother arrived and ordered them to dig to the bottom of the cave, but Bahram was not there either and the excavated soil of the mountain remained untouched around this cave. The poem ends with a word play about the homonyms of *gur*, which can mean both the wild ass and the tomb. In passing, there is a hint regarding the difficult times through which Ganja went when the poem was written.

The base are sated by dust / Vassals are forced down by
a heavy hand

Despite the complexity of the poem's structure, its sections are remarkably welded together. It is of course impossible in this condensed account to present all the details, but it is worth mentioning, nevertheless, how the motives mirror one another seamlessly: the construction of the Khavarnak and the construction of the seven pavilions, Nu'man's repentance and Bahram's secret disappearance. Particularly interesting are the seven stories, which match the colours and depict increasingly enlightening image of love, starting with crude lust and ending with love as a union for for conjugal life. On top of all their richness and beauty, the stories also reveal possible ways to interpret Nizami's perception of Sufi morals.

One might notice, for instance, that Nizami remained true to his principles and refused to follow in Firdawsi's footsteps. Here, like in his previous poems, he used elements of the past always following the same aim. The poem should not serve merely for artistic pleasure, but it must also teach, and above all it must inculcate wise government of the country. The history of Bahram in the main episodes serves as an illustration of the situation that was already described in the *Treasury of Secrets*. Despite his old age, Nizami did not soften his tone regarding government. He highlighted the corruption of the court nobility, and the impotence of even the just ruler himself, surrounded by traitorous and greedy predators. He called on the old cattleman to teach wisdom to the ruler by letting him know his views openly and plainly. Yet it is characteristic that all the advice and the admonitions given in the poem do not take the shape of dry and insipid exhortations, as it is usually the case in Near Eastern literature, but they are clothed in sharp full-blooded artistic colours which leave a long-standing impression in readers' minds and predispose them to accept the central arguments of the poem.

Thus, the great master succeeded in achieving this complex and difficult task and created a work whose colours have not faded right up to the present day, and which continues to delight generation after generation with its perfection..

Work: The Iskandar-nama

As we have seen above, the last and most extensive of his poems is the one in which Nizami invested the most work. At the end of his life, the poet wanted to gather all his life experience, to unite all his broad knowledge in one unique creation.The figure of Alexander of Macedon was perfect for this purpose. The link between Alexander and Aristotle, who was for the medieval Near East the ultimate representative of ancient Greek philosophy, gave him the opportunity to include in the poem extensive sections dedicated to different philosophical theories.

The portrayal of Alexander as a master of the arts allowed the poet to introduce further expressive art in his poem. Most important for Nizami, Alexander was the ideal ruler incarnate, an enlightened and moral authority, and thus, more than in any other of his creations, the poet could expand on the themes about which he was so concerned: the governance of the world.

These themes had attracted attention long before Nizami in the East as well as in the West. It does not come as a surprise that almost, if not all, people of the world were so deeply influenced by the figure of Alexander as a conqueror, who united under his power all the world's cultures of his time, distinguishing himself with amazing beauty and ended his life in his prime, at the peak of his knowledge. In all likelihood, Alexander's legend was already created and developed in the fourth century B.C.E. and the warfare conducted by his Diadochi throughout his empire was the first propagation of these legends. Beside the legends, an official biography of Alexander was established early on by Cleitarchus and Onesicritus, which was used later on as material for Plutarch's work (50-120 C.E.), which influenced considerably the formation of novels about Alexander on the European continent.

Yet if his supporters and sometime enthusiastic admirers hallowed their hero, his enemies, the aristocratic families of the regions conquered by Alexander, equally could not remain indifferent. Among them an apocryphal literature started to be developed, in order to rehabilitate the defeated and to remove the shame of their defeat. It was a difficult task. Alexander's victories were popular and trying to deny them was futile, so the proponents of this literature chose an alternative method. They started to deny the Macedonian origins of Alexander, and in diverse ways tried to link him with native traditions. They made him one of their ancestors by blood, and thus, in accordance with the theories of legitimation of that time, in a manner of speaking negated the fact if the conquest. Alexander ceased to be a conqueror as he took only that which he was entitled to take. Consequently, the honour of the dynasty was not threatened and theocratic principles remained untouched. This version of events was often favoured in the East until quite late in history. Hence the example of the spurious genealogy of the famous Sultan Mahmud of Ghazni, who established his connection to the Sasanians, and in this way was able to placate the pride of the native Iranian aristocracy which had been shaken by the victory of the "son of a Turkish slave".

One of the oldest works of this kind, presenting a biography of Alexander woven with legends, is the famous Greek Alexander Romance. This was ascribed to Alexander's doctor, Callisthenes, with whom it did not have any actual connection, for which reason it has been called in European scholarship, Pseudo-Callisthenes. The story originates in the first century C.E., subsequently enjoying success around the world.

One might consider as a proven fact that the novel derives from an Egyptian original. This is clear even though in the Egyptian version Alexander was the son of an Egyptian priest Nektaneb, who used magical powers to seduce the wife of King Philip. Obviously the novel must also have been of primary interest for Iran in particular. Alexander's invasion brought about the end of the Achaemenid dynasty and came as a severe blow for the Magi, the Zoroastrian clergy, who played a prominent role in pre-Islamic Iran. It is then quite logical that Alexander appeared as the most evil enemy, destroyer and tyrant from a Zoroastrian perspective. A typical example is for instance Hamza al-Isfahani (d. c. 970), who seized the opportunity to use for his "History of the Kings and the Prophets" a wide range of historical works about Alexander put together in native Iranian aristocratic circles. In touching upon Alexander's construction activities and stories about the twelve "Alexandrias", he concludes the passage, with these words: "But there are no grounds for this, he might have been a conqueror, but he was certainly not a constructor!" One of the books which has been preserved to the present day in Middle Persian presents Alexander as follows: "The evil Ahriman, wishing to shake the faith, instigated the unrighteous Alexander the Byzantine, who lived in Egypt, to go to Iranshahr, bringing heavy persecutions, war and destruction. He killed the Iranian ruler, and then ruined and devastated the capital and the country... and killed many... Mobeds . . . and guardians of the faith and nobles and wise men of Iranshah. Among the leaders and the householders of Iranshah, he kindled animosity and enmity between them, and he died and was cast in hell."

This hostility did not diminish the desire to gather as much information as possible regarding the enemy. In later periods, Iran maintained this tactic and thoroughly studied the history of the Arab conquerors and even later on, the Mongols. Hence it does not come as a surprise that the Pseudo-Callisthenes was translated from Greek into Pahlavi already between the second and the fourth centuries.

This translation was not preserved, like most of the Middle Persian literature. Yet a Syriac version did survive, which. as is clear from the text, had been translated from Pahlavi, and not from the Greek original. This can be observed through the transliteration of the proper names, which, in Syriac version, always appear with Iranian characters, as well as many other details. One only needs to consider some particular features, such as the description of the peoples, who stood out against Nektaneb. In the Greek text, one can see the following nations: Indians, Evonimites, Oksidraki, Iberians, Caucones, Aellopods, Bosphorians, Bastarnae, Azan and Chalybes. Among all the fantasy and the exoticism of some of these names, most of them are characteristically Hellenistic. The Syriac version of this passage presents the following peoples: Turays, Alans, Gubarbedays, Armenians, Belsays, Alasays, Shabronkays, Midians, Arabs, Midianites, Azerbaijanis, Alinikays, Galates, Tabaristi, Gurgani and Khaldeys. Without going too deeply into the analysis of this passage, it is possible to establish at first glance that the author could not have translated the Hellenistic version. And it is particularly astonishing that the names in the Syriac version refer mostly to people of the Caucasus and the precincts of the Caspian Sea. The author must have been familiar with the names of these regions.

The Syriac version was reproduced several times in the same language, and these versions reached Arabic literature, which, as it is generally agreed, used the Syriac translation considerably at the beginning of the Caliphate.

To the Syriac version, a reference is added to Dhul Qarnayn from the Quran (Q. 18/82). The Quran commentators, when explaining this verse, point to the clear resemblance with the main features of the legend. Ibn Khurdadba reports that a man called Sallam, who was a translator in 842-4 under the caliphate of Wasiq, went to the Great Wall of China, which could indicate the desire to verify the information, given in the legend.

However, apart from the fact that the whole romance has obviously not been translated into the Arabic language, the old chronicles do not preserve the tradition fully and therefore establishing its sources is impossible. The furthest one might go in this regard is probably our current level of knowledge about the texts. When Sasanian historiography started establishing the official version of the history of the royal family and its ancestors, in other words the famous "Book of Kings"(Khuday-namag), it was the translation in Pahlavi of Pseudo-Callisthenes that was used. To limit it to a damnation of Alexander was impossible as there was no way of denying his conquest of Iran, so it was necessary to justify that circumstance. The author of the chronicle starts in the same way as Pseudo-Callisthenes did, but while the Egyptian version presented Alexander as Egyptian, the Iranian aristocracy had to find for him Iranian origins. This was achieved by establishing a legend, according to which Alexander was the son of a daughter of Philip and the Achaemenid Darius, but adopted as a son by Philip. The purpose of the creation of this legend is obvious, If Alexander was Darius' son, i.e. an Achaemenid, then the prestige of the Iranian royal dynasty was not affected by the conquest. He possessed farr, a hereditary grace that only princes of Iranian blood could obtain, and therefore had the right to sit on the Achaemenid throne.

This version of the legend was then translated into Arabic and it is this text that Firdawsi used for his *Shah-nama*. Yet obviously, aside from the Arabic and the Persian versions, the *Shah-nama* also perpetuated the transmission of local traditions, for the details of the Arabic chronicle do not appear either in Firdawsi's text or in the versions known to us from before Islam. Hence, Tabari stated that Alexander died in Shahrazur (which is close to Nizami's version of events), Mas'udi mentioned the meeting between Alexander and the Indian prince Keydi, who corresponds with Nizami's Keyda.

Caucasian peoples also had their version. The Pseudo-Callisthenes inspired an Armenian narrative, and Movses Khorenatsi's chronicle shows the author's familiarity with his own local traditions. Thus when Nizami engaged himself with his last task, the Alexander novel already had its own history, parts of which were undoubtedly rooted in the Caucasus, so that it reinforced more strongly the link of the conqueror with this region. One might think that again, as was the case for *Khusraw and Shirin*, the starting point for Nizami was Firdawsi's poem, against which he could present his critique. This is at least what appears in the following verses:

That earlier poet, the wise man from Tus / Who ornamented speech's face like a bride

In that poem where he pierced pearls / He left many things unsaid that ought to be expressed

He did not say what did not suit him / But only what he had to

These verses did not emerge by chance. Nizami noticed rightly that Firdawsi did not write "that which he did not want", i.e. in order to protect his political conscience, he considered it acceptable to remain silent on some details of the legend, which he nevertheless must have known.

The link with Firdawsi and the old epic traditions appears again in the metre that Nizami chose for this poem. He selected a metre that he had not used previously, and it is the favourite of epic poetry from the golden age of Persian poetry, which is called *mutaqarib* and can be schematised as follows:

$$\cup - - \mid \cup - - \mid \cup - - \mid \cup -$$

Nevertheless, one should never imagine that Nizami set himself the task to produce a new variant of Firdawsi's poem, in other words, that the *Iskandar-nama* is simply a new version of the *Shah-nama*. While preparing for the creation of this poem, Nizami invested a considerable amount of work, which he mentioned quite clearly in the introduction of the poem.

I have not seen the feats of that king, who traversed the world / Written in a single scroll

Words, locked away like treasure, / Were scattered throughout every manuscript

I gathered the essence from every manuscript / And garbed it in the ornament of verse

Apart from recent histories / Jewish, Christian and Pahlavi,

I collected what was fine in every work / And skinned every parchment for its marrow

Most importantly here is the triplet of established traditions that Nizami is using. While Firdawsi built his entire work on Sasanian conceptions, which matched his own vision, Nizami, on the other hand, was living in a region of much closer contact between Muslims and Christians, i.e. Georgians and Armenians, and thus he did not want, nor could he neglect, their perspectives. Through these traditions, an alternative view on the Antique world was laid before him. Many pages of this poem speak clearly to the fact that ancient Greek philosophy was known to him not only through Aristotelianism in its Islamic guise which was widely spread across the lands of the Caliphate already in the tenth century, but also in another light, in the form that was preserved in ancient monasteries in Georgia and Armenia, about whose lives Nizami knew so much. This gives his poem about Alexander particular value, and makes it a monument that stands apart among the literatures of the lands of the former Caliphate.

Before turning our attention to a short presentation of the poem's content, it is worth briefly mentioning its title, which underwent many distortions at the whim of the scribes, and has led to considerable discord among authors who have written about Nizami. The poem is divided into two books of different sizes (the first of them being considerably longer). Both parts appear under the general title of the *Iskandar-nama*, yet each of them has its own subtitle. The first one, as it can be seen in its introduction, is the poem itself called *Sharaf-nama*, the book of glory, distinction, honour, for it describes Alexander's ascent towards glory.

The second part does not have such a precise name. Most of the time, it is called *Khirad-nama*, the book of reason, following the first words with which it starts, but it is also known under the name of *Iqbal-nama*, the book of happiness or success. However, some authors attribute this name to the first part of the poem (Hajji Khalifa). The reason for this lies in the fact that there was no strict tradition, and the scribes changed the title at their own discretion. It is worth adding here that some old sources named the first part "land" (*barri*) and the second one "sea" (*bahri*), as the second part narrates Alexander's travels by sea.

After the usual introduction, Nizami starts the poem with a chapter dedicated to a short overview of the whole poem. Then comes a chapter inviting the reader to pay attention to this poem. Such a lengthy introduction is not seen in the previous poems, which indicates the particular significance that the poet attached to his final work.

Nizami wanted to show his main character in three aspects: as a ruler, as a philosopher and as a prophet.

> *Some call him the possessor of a throne / A nation-builder, even a world-conqueror*
>
> *Others, on account of his governance / Have written a decree in the name of his wisdom*
>
> *Yet others, recalling his pure spirit and his piety / Have accepted him as a prophet*
>
> *From each of the three seeds scattered by a wise man / I shall plant a fruit-bearing tree*
>
> *First I will knock on kingship's door / And speak of how he conquered the world*
>
> *Then I shall devote my speech to wisdom / Engaging once more with old perplexions*
>
> *Then I will hammer on the door of prophet-hood / Since God too called him a prophet*
>
> *I have built three doors, each the entrance to a treasure mine / In turn I have laboured on each door*
>
> *Through these three doors, or these three pearls / I will fill the skirts of the world will treasure*

Nizami mentions three parts, but as we have seen above, there are only two. This is due to the fact that the second and the third parts are actually merged into one, for Nizami could not separate wisdom from the prophet, and possibly, for other reasons which it is not possible to cover here. As for the construction one can already detect a significant difference from Firdawsi, who regarded Alexander almost exclusively as a hero.

Nizami begins his narration with the question of Alexander's origins. He refers to the "story of the *dihqans*", i.e. the legend established by the Iranian aristocracy according to which Alexander was a son of Darius, and consequently, a legal successor to the Iranian throne. Yet the purpose of the creation of this legend is clear for the poet. He rejects it with indignation as an empty narrative. Instead, he proposes another story, according to which Alexander was the son of a hermit beggar adopted by Philip who found him on the cadaver of his mother who had died in the cold. However, even this version does not satisfy the poet who is inclined to present Alexander simply as Philip's son. It is worth noticing here though that the name 'Philip' appears in a corrupt form in all copies as 'Philiqus', which probably came about through the addition of a superfluous dot above the second letter 'fa', turning it into a 'qaf', in the Arabized form of the name, 'Filifus'.

Considerable attention is given to the story of Alexander's education and training, as he studied with the future great scholar Aristotle at his father's palace. A short description of Alexander's ascent to the throne and his oath to always strive for justice and the happiness of his subjects marks the beginning of the narrative about his campaigns. His conquests are typically not motivated by the desire to increase his power or expand his territory, but on the contrary, they derive from the attempt to help those who have been humiliated and oppressed.

A messenger arrived from Egypt asking Alexander's help against the Zanji, i.e. the inhabitants of Zanzibar, or the black people, who were laying waste to the Nile valley, and Alexander set out. The war was particularly challenging, for the numbers of the Zanji were greater, and in addition, they were bloodthirsty cannibals, who inspired fear among the Macedonians. But Alexander adopted military cunning and made the Zanji believe that his army was also cannibalistic; he instilled terror in them and showed marvelous courage in single combat with their leader, and in the end achieved a spectacular victory. To appease Egypt, he built Alexandria and sent to Darius, to whom his father paid tribute, countless gifts from the booty of the war. However Darius disregarded this and Alexander decided to cut his relationship with him, refusing to pay further tribute. Trusting in the divination which had promised him a favourable future, Alexander prepared himself for war.

A small story is introduced here about the invention of the mirror. It should be mentioned at this point that descriptions usually linked Alexander with a mirror possessing the miraculous function of reflecting everything that was happening in the world. Nizami knew about this legend, but he refused the fantastic elements and he explained this legend as simply the discovery of a normal metal mirror.

Then Darius' ambassadors arrived. They brought to Alexander as mockery, the following gifts from the Iranian sovereign, a ball, a *chawgan*, i.e. a polo mallet, and sesame seeds. This must have meant that Alexander was still a child who should amuse himself with toys. The sesame seeds symbolised the innumerable Iranian army. But Alexander interpreted these gifts in his own way. The mallet was given to him as a hook for Iranian kingship. The ball was the earth, over which the young Macedonian was going to rule. As for the sesame seeds, they were thrown to the birds that promptly ate all the grains. Instead of presents, Alexander sent to Darius a measure of the bitter and acidic seeds of the rue plant, so bitter and acidic that nobody could eat them, not even birds, and they could, it was believed, badly damage the eyes. Both sides prepared for war, which started with an extremely spectacular and arrogant letter from Darius and a proud and quiet reply from Alexander.

After a battle before Mosul, two Iranian noblemen came to Alexander and offered to kill Darius for a good reward. Alexander thought that Darius' death could save the life of an immeasurable number of innocent people and he gave his consent. The following day he received the news that Darius had been killed. Nevertheless, he did not rejoice at the news, but rushed to the defeated ruler of Iran and supported him during his death throes. The scene of their meeting is portrayed with incredible strength. The author gives a very tangible description of the ire and the cruel sense of powerlessness of the dying Darius. The killers received the reward promised to them, but as vile traitors they were condemned to a shameful death.

Alexander assumed rule of the country and published an edict, promising the population mercy and justice. The Zoroastrian priests were the only ones to suffer, for the *ateshgah* (fire temples) were destroyed everywhere.

According to the promise he gave to Darius, he took his daughter, the beautiful Rawshanak (Roxana), as his wife. He solemnly entered Istakhr, Iran's capital city, to take the throne. Foreseeing his future campaigns, he sent his young wife with Aristotle to Greece.

Then follows a famous Muslim interpretation of Alexander's journey to the Ka'ba and his circumambulation around the shrine. At this time came a messenger from Azerbaijan, calling him to the Caucasus. He went to Armenia and from there to Abkhazia, over which a certain Duval was ruling. In Georgia, Alexander built Ti is, which Nizami describes as an earthly paradise. He was then told that Barda'a was governed by a powerful queen named Nushaba (called Qaydafa by Firdawsi and Kandake by Pseudo-Callisthenes). She was keeping in her court only women and would not allow men to come to her. The kingdom of this courageous and just sovereign was thriving and Alexander was particularly touched by the extraordinary natural beauty of these places. Nizami proudly exalts the beauty of his own country. Having received a gift from Nushaba, Alexander decided to visit her under the guise of an ambassador.

Here comes again a scene with particularly fine psychological description. Alexander entered the throne chamber, without bending his head or laying down his sword as ambassadors usually did. His words were bold and self-assured and the queen guessed that only Alexander could talk like this, letting him know that she had recognised him. Alexander was getting ready to sell his life dearly but Nushaba did not want enemies in Macedonia. After amusing entertainment, when Alexander was given precious stones instead of food, they made peace and as a sign of conciliation, the queen invited him to a grandiose banquet.

The whole episode is complemented by ancient legends about the amazons, yet it cannot be doubted that Nushaba's image is influenced by the information that Nizami had about Queen Tamara, whose praises he sings also in his second poem.

Alexander then embarked on a long journey. His aim was to know where people were living more happily than anywhere else and to destroy oppression and injustice everywhere in the world. With the help of a hermit, he conquered the castle of Derbent, where an intractable ruler was governing, robbing and plundering the villages and settlements all around. After the conquest of Derbent, Alexander built a wall, which was meant to protect the harvest from the Kipchak robbers who constituted a considerable threat.

He visited the castle of Sarir, where stood the throne of Kay Khusraw and the famous cup of Jamshid. Yet he did not try to obtain these sacred objects, he simply sat on the throne and drank from the cup. Bulinas (Apollonius), who was accompanying him, read the inscription on the cup and the first astrolabe was created based on its image. In a cave where Kay Khusraw once mysteriously disappeared, he found sulphur deposits. After Khorasan and Ray, he went to India. King Kayd, having received his letter, sent him a present. Having secured safe passage he crossed Tibet to reach China and despite some friction, he succeeded in establishing peaceful relationship with the Khaqan. This section contains a particularly interesting chapter about the competition between Greek and Chinese artists, which played a tremendous role in the art history of the Near East. The author also introduces the legendary story of the artist Mani, the famous founder of Manicheism.

On his way back, Alexander founded Samarkand and headed then to Greece when suddenly a messenger came from Armenia with terrible news. The Abkhaz Duval informed him that the Rus had attacked Barda'a, destroyed everything and plundered Nushaba's kingdom. This obvious anachronism illustrates the desire to depict an event which was apparently felt very strongly in the Caucasus, i.e. the Russian invasion of Barda'a which occurred around 1170. A Russian fleet of about 72-73 vessels sailed down the Volga to the Caspian and then up the Kura. At the same time, obviously in agreement with the invaders, the Khazars captured Derbent and Shabaran castle. The Shirvanshah's own army could not compete with the enemy and sought help from the Georgian king, Georgi III. The Khazars were expelled, and the Russian fleet seems to have perished in a storm on the Caspian Sea.[20]

With the description of this war, Nizami succeeded in giving a very strong impression of the Rus, who in his words, were bold and fierce fighters with whom it was not easy to deal. Heading towards Barda'a, Alexander crossed the Kipchak steppe. More than ever, he was stunned by the beauty of Kipchak women. He feared that his army, longing for female affection on campaign, would resort to violence. He tried to convince the Kipchak leaders that they should force their women to hide their faces. They rejected this proposition with indignation: their women were free; enslaving them was not possible. Only by cunning could Alexander reach his objective and manage to avoid clashes with the population.

Undoubtedly, this episode was brought to Nizami's mind by memories of first wife, the lovely Afaq, whose love for freedom and beauty were constantly present in many verses of his poem. Once he arrived there, Alexander realised that fighting back the Rus was not an easy task. Their leader, Kintal, was bold and unflinching, although presumptuous and boastful. Alexander needed to build a whole coalition with various peoples who would all be willing to fight. His only advantage was that the military techniques of the Rus were not as advanced as those of the Greeks. Nonetheless, to gain victory he had to go through seven difficult and dangerous battles the descriptions of which occupy central passages of the poem. In the end, he succeeded and he freed his friend Nushaba. Here there is an interesting reference to the fact that the Rus were using fur (sable, marten) instead of money.

Thereupon begins the concluding section of the poem. Alexander found out from conversations with the inhabitants of the country that in the land of eternal darkness towards the North Pole, there is a spring of the water of life. Whoever drinks from it will stay young and live forever. Alexander decided to undertake this new and difficult challenge. The road was long and difficult and his army suffered, but they finally reached this frightening land. Yet Alexander did not risk entering the darkness, fearing that they would not be able to find the way back. The difficulty was solved by an old man, who advised him to take with him a filly, whose newly born foal would stay in the camp. For a filly will always find its way to its foal.

Alexander however could not find the spring in the dark. He looked for it forty days, until a mysterious voice declared to him that his strength would not carry him to his aim. This voice advised him to take a small stone from the land of darkness and weigh it once in the light. Thanks to the precious enlightening stone, al-Khizr who was leading his army managed to find the spring and he received eternal life. Nizami acknowledged here that in the lands of Rum they told the story differently. Al-Khizr wandered in the darkness with Ilyas (Elijah)/ By chance, they sat down to eat beside a spring, the nature of which they did not know. Some salt fish that they were eating fell in the water and were revived in it. This is how they discovered that the water was rejuvenating.

Once out of the darkness, Alexander tried to weigh the stone he got from there. But a hundred mountains put on the scale could not match it. The only weight which worked was a handful of dust. This is a symbol of human greed. Only a handful of earth from the grave could sate the greedy gaze of humans.

Alexander returned and on the way he managed to discover a secret city, the inhabitants of which could from time to time call forth a voice that resonated from a mountain nearby. They climbed up there, but were never seen again. Sending the army there did not achieve anything. It set off but never came back. This gloomy episode is the conclusion of the first part.

The second part begins with a story about how, on his return to Byzantium, Alexander arranged the treasures he brought back with him. He ordered the translation of the works of wise men that he had obtained, such as the Persian book of kings, the description of the world, and the description of the world of spirits. Thereafter he convened wise men from all around the world and concerned himself with the promotion of science. Close to his capital city, he built for himself a solitary cell, where he could go when he needed rest from the people and give time to his thoughts. This part serves as an introduction to ten stories, which come undoubtedly from Greek sources. It is not possible to list them all here and so the following description presents only the most interesting ones.

The second section is dedicated to the question of Alexander's epithet in the East: Zu al-Qarnayn, the possessor of two horns, for which there are a wide range of old explanations, including the famous Quranic mention (Q.18:82), which derives from a Syrian legend of the seventh century. Nizami transposes onto Alexander the well-known ancient Greek myth about Midas. The fourth section is a curious one, which presents the love of Archimedes and clearly draws its sources from outside the Muslim world. This section contains the praise of monogamy, already mentioned above. The last sections are devoted to Greek sages, in particular Hermes Trismegistus, the magical power of music and the conversation between Alexander and Diogenes.

These introductory chapters are followed by a part in which Nizami demonstrates Alexander's philosophical abilities. It starts with a scientific discussion between the king and an Indian student who asks him questions. The topics of these questions, from the finitude or the infinitude of the universe to the incarnation of the soul, and from the significance of dreams to the relevance of astrology as a science, were undoubtedly burning problems, in which all intellectuals of the twelfth century were interested. This part is present in the Greek original version (as a conversation with the Indian gymnosophists), yet Nizami substitutes the problems with questions that are more interesting for him.

A dispute starts in front of Alexander around the discussion on the origin of the world between seven renowned Greek thinkers: Aristotle, Apollonius of Tyana, Socrates, Plato, Thales, Porphyrus and Hermes. As is clear from the list, Nizami is not too concerned with chronology; it is not important for him to present the history of philosophy, but rather to present all the most important and famous Ancient Greek theories. The poetic level of this section is, of course, lower than the usual level of Nizami's verses, but they are exceptionally interesting in showing the exceptionally rich thought of Western philosophy which were far from common knowledge among Muslim thinkers, yet were mastered perfectly by the great poet. The conclusion introduces his own views on the question, which shows that he held gnostic-Neoplatonic beliefs.

Alexander grew step by step in human awareness to the highest possible level. A mysterious voice then called him and announced that he has been chosen for a prophetic mission. He must awaken humanity and call it to pursue the way towards the knowledge of good.

You must build this old vault anew / And rid the horizon of ignorance

Rid the earth of demonic injustice / And turn it towards the Lord of the World

Lift the heads of the sleeping from sleep / And the veil from the face of wisdom

Alexander, as he received this order, decided to depart again for a long pilgrimage. This time, he needed another kind of weapon: wisdom. The philosophers Aristotle, Plato and Socrates established for him "books of wisdom", of which Nizami provides some excerpts. These books contain all Nizami's worldviews in compressed aphoristic form, his teachings, exposed in a dry, and, for him unusually, highly moralistic tone.

Alexander set off and went to Alexandria, from there to Jerusalem, and following the African coast, he reached Spain (Andalusia). Then with his companions he embarked on a boat which took them to the western edge of the world, where the sun sets in the vast ocean. He found there stones that provoke laughter so uncontrollable that people can die from it. With them, he built an impregnable castle in an oasis. After six months of wanderings in the desert, Alexander returned to Africa and travelled to the South to find the source of the Nile. It is interesting that Nizami mentions these sources, which in the 19th Century cost the lives of so many Europeans.

The western expedition is followed by a journey to southern countries. It is worth noticing here the both region in which the inhabitants were addicted to opium and who were cured of this addiction by Alexander, and the valleys of diamonds and precious stones. This part ends with glorification of the toil of the farmer.

From the southern countries, Alexander headed to the East. He visited India, destroying temples everywhere; and he arrived in China. With the help of the Chinese emperor, with whom he had concluded an agreement previously, he undertook a journey to the sea. On the sea shore, he saw the beautiful singing mermaids, the Homeric sirens. With some of his closest companions, Alexander went by boat across the sea to explore its wonders. They reached the place where the sea fell into the "world ocean". One could not go further and to warn sailors about the danger, Alexander placed a copper statue with raised hands indicating that one should not carry on beyond this point.

After some dangers on their way back, the travellers reached China, where they rested for a month and then departed for their longer journey. They headed to the North. There, they encountered a population afraid of the attacks of the warriors of the Yajuj tribe. To defend them, Alexander built an immense wall that restricted the passage of these warriors and was strong enough to stand until the Day of Judegement. This is a legend whose origins must be connected with reports about the Great Wall of China, which were circulating in the Near East.

On the way, Alexander arrived in a country with a heavenly climate and abundance of fruit and crops. Through discussions with its inhabitants, he understood that he had finally discovered the country of eternal happiness, for which he had been searching such a long time. There were no lies, no robbery and no violence in it. No oppressed or oppressive people were living there, nor rich or poor. People were equal to each other; they considered themselves as brothers and were ready to do anything to help each other. Therefore they needed neither rulers nor representatives of authority and even the flocks did not need shepherds. They were moderate in their way of life, hence they did not know of any diseases and they lived to a very advanced age before leaving the world with peace of mind.

Alexander was deeply struck. The ideal country, about which he had dreamt, revealed itself before him. He said that if he had known about the existence of this city, he would not have wandered around the world, but he would have chosen this exemplary way of life and made it his own path.

This grandiose depiction shows the dream that this great poet cherished all his life. Looking aross the content of his poems, it becomes clear that all the depictions of modes of governance have one goal: indicating the path to this wonderful country, a country of equality and fraternity, the harmonious calmness of which cannot be disrupted. Nizami must have truly believed that this ideal was achievable on earth. For him, this was a dream, a beautiful yet elusive dream. The conditions of his time did not allow him to outline the ways in which it would be possible to bring this ideal closer. But the simple description of this scene at the end of the last poem of this great author indicates that Nizami wanted to express his last words, notwithstanding the risk, in opposition to the terrible world of violence and cruelty, and to support a world of harmonious justice for a liberated population. Furthermore, excitement seizes us, happy sons of the great Socialist homeland, thinking that Nizami placed this country in the north! The invisible ties that link the twelfth century to our life, that relate us to the great creator allow us to affirm that if he was living out in the present day, he would have been on our side! His dream was achieved and we owe thanks to Nizami for this dream achieved by similar, albeit later, 'dreamers' who gave their life fearlessly to build a better future for humanity.

Alexander saw that which could be achieved on earth and then, the mysterious voice ordered him to quickly return. Crossing via Kerman, he reached Babylon, and from there headed towards Rome, but in Shahrazur he became sick, which at first he attributed to the action of poison. Autumn came, and Alexander felt that he had reached the end. Scholars had no power to help him and during a moment of strength he mocked their lack of power. In his last hours, he asked for a scribe and dictated to him a letter to his mother, to announce his death. He asked her, however, not to grieve and mourn him. If she wanted to have a burial ceremony, then she could organise a funeral and invite only those who had never had a close relative die. Having sent the letter, he struggled a short while and died with a smile on his face. His body was solemnly carried to Alexandria and buried in a crypt.

This scene is followed by a short concluding chapter, dedicated to the destiny of the hero's kin and the seven wise men. The nobiltiy wanted to put Iskandarus on the throne, but he refused it, replying that successors to his great father in this world did not exist. The destiny of the seven wise men is then shortly summarised, including quite a detailed account of Socrates. Answering the question of his students as to where his body should be buried, he replied that it does not matter to him where his bones lie.

On this gloomy tone ends the last poem of this great author. This short chapter cannot give a complete enough description, and only the main points have been described. Yet this is sufficient to understand that, although some claim it as Nizami's weakest poem, the author stands here at an incredibly high level. It is true that there are none of the dramatic encounters which embellish *Khusraw and Shirin* or *Layla and Majnun*, but the task was entirely different. Here, Nizami stands as a teacher and a thinker, and he gathered together everything that tormented and moved him in his life. Therefore, this poem might be the most priceless material for the understanding of Nizami's personal views, the breadth of his knowledge and his love for humankind, which warmed his heart all his life. The study of this work is still ongoing and it it necessary to explore further Nizami's sources, in order to clarify the new elements that he inserted into this beautiful ancient story.

Lyric Works

When one mentions Nizami, first in mind are his extraordinary poems, which have been briefly presented above. It is normally forgotten that Nizami was also an unequalled master of precise and elegant lyrics. Unfortunately, it is very difficult to characterise his works in this regard, for the manuscripts of his lyric divan (collection of poems), although some are available to us, are rare and almost unstudied. Today, the famous manuscripts of his divan are in the Bodleian library, in Oxford (England), one in Berlin, one in Cairo and two in India. Isolated ghazals can also be found in anthologies. Editing and carrying out critical research on this collection are difficult, but they are necessary, and this will hopefully happen quicker thanks to the approaching celebration of Nizami's jubilee.

For now, it is only possible to note the following regarding his lyric works. Although old sources affirm that the number of Nizami's poems was high, this is apparently not true. The collections which have been preserved contain usually about two thousands lines, which is most likely the main part of the collection. It is currently impossible to establish the date of its completion. Even though one might think that most of the ghazals were written when the poet was still young, there are some poems in which Nizami talks about his old age. Consequently, he did not stop writing lyric poems until the end. Naturally, compared to his long poems, they occupied at that time quite a minor position within his oeuvre.

There is no doubt that the poems which survive now belong to Nizami. Each of their verses exhibits exactly the same extraordinary mastery that is so characteristic of his magical words. It is possible to say that, in the divan as well as in the poems, there is no verse which does not contain this artistic quality, polished like a precious stone. To the objection that in the twelfth century the level of technical skill required for poets was extremely high, one can reply that Nizami's contemporaneous poets, Khaqani and Falaki are not less accomplished in terms of form. This is absolutely true. However, it must be said that for Khaqani and Falaki this pursuit of sophistication was the main objective.

Such verses cannot be found in Nizami's collection of works. His prodigious artistic talent, coupled with the boldness of his creativity, never allowed him to go beyond the boundaries of artistic perfection. Surprisingly, Nizami wrote in his whole life more than a hundred thousand verses. When divided equally across his life, this means that he wrote about ten verses per day. But as shown above, there was no such even distribution: his longest poem contains fourteen thousand verses and it was written in a year or less. He did not have time, therefore, to reflect on each single verse, to reread, rewrite and polish that which he wrote. How gifted, then, this extraordinary poet must have been, considering that it is impossible to find any technical weakness in the whole of his oeuvre! This miracle is inexplicable, as each thought must have come to him in its artistic form. I myself have struggled to find a parallel to this phenomenon in world literature. There is no scale on which to measure Nizami - he can be measured only against his own standards.

Most of the divan lyrics are concerned with love. They deal with deep passion, but also the tender and pure expression of a fervent heart; a heart that is able to love more than any individual has ever been able to. This profound and intrinsic love does not seek anything for itself; it finds delight in giving itself fully to another. As the author expressed it:

I mix my heart with yours, since your soul is mingled with mine / I would need another soul to have another lover

Nizami's ghalzals, as most lyric compositions of this (and later) periods, allow a Sufi interpretation, but should this necessarily be so? It is a fundamental question. His love for Afaq, his beloved friend, was a love which even in his old age was still burning vividly in his heart. It seems to me that the extraordinary sincerity, the graciousness of his ghazals fits poorly into abstract and scholarly Sufi theories. They are not needed here, because before our eyes the intimate secrets of the soul of a great individual are exposed.

It is worth mentioning one more characteristic of these poems. It is well known that artistic methods in the Near East do not require from ghazals any thematic unity. On the contrary, each *bayt* (two verses) must constitute a whole, linked to another *bayt* only through rhythm and metre. This gives to the ghazals a distinctive broken quality and for us weakens the artistic force of the poem. Even in the ghazals of a great master like Hafiz it is very unusual to find an impression of unity. Mostly, the alternation of verses within the ghazals does not have a significant influence on the general structure. In contrast to this, Nizami composed each ghazal as a complete entity following a specific plan that develops a single proposition on a central motif. Each of his ghazals could be given a title to summarise its topic, which is almost impossible with Hafiz for instance.

Here is as an example one of his ghazals which comes from a beautiful old anthology kept in one of the Istanbul libraries:

> *The punishment of a night without you is punishment indeed / A breath of regret taken without you is regret indeed*
>
> *In the inevitability of union, since I cannot evade you / In the repose of your hair, since I feel repose only with you*

I dare not imagine searching for one like you / That you should search for one like me - I have no such hope

Near me you appear great, and I - small / Before me you are mighty, and I – mean

I have no eyes to see you, nor luck to find you / No legs to run to you, nor hands to raise to you

You are beyond Nizami, yet I search for you / My days are spent in fortune-telling, and my nights in counting stars

Such unity in structure is also seen in the following ghazal from the same collection:

Why do you abuse an old friend like me? / My God, the things you say! How elegantly you keep faith with me.

Leave me with my regret. If you ask me of it / Do not fret my name like this, if you would fret

Whatever shape you chose, I will chose it too / Even if you count rosary beads and wear the Christian's belt

I love you yet you revile me / You honour me yet I disgust you

Nizami considers you dear to him at all times / Does it become you, his beloved, to hold him in contempt?

Rendering the beauty of the original poem in translation is of course impossible. Yet it seems to me that it is not easy to find another poet who could convey even approximately the restrained fervour, the soft reproach which is invoked in these wonderful verses. Each of their words is music, but not a loud symphonic orchestra - a barely audible rustling whisper of the *tar*, the gentle sound of a flute in the moonlight, wafting through the vineyards. It is clear that apart from Nizami, the greatest singer of love songs, no one else could produce similar lyrics, which do not fade or get lost even alongside the dazzling paintings of his longer poems.

Language and Technical Mastery

I n the concluding chapter of this work it is necessary to mention a brief word about the particular characteristics of the great poet's technical mastery. This could easily be the topic of a whole essay, so a full demonstration of the splendour of his artistic strength is not the intention here, but merely a general and superficial impression of the technical methods of his poetry.

First of all, it is necessary to mention that the tradition established two centuries before Nizami required that epic poetry use a simplified archaic language. This trend appeared with the Shu'ubiyya movement among the native Iranian aristocracy, in a genre championed by them and unknown to their Arab conquerors, in order to reflect pre-Islamic Iranian traditions.

We have already seen how decisively Nizami rejects the self-glorification of the Iranian nobility as its helplessness was clear to him. He did not think it necessary to support their claim to power nor to strengthen the legendary position invented by them, and he preferred to courageously highlight their idleness.

His relationship to language flows quite logically from this starting point. If the conditions of the time forced him to use Persian literary language, he nevertheless saw it as completely useless to employ archaisms to strive for an imagined purity. He used Arabic words boldly when they allowed him to enrich his language, or enhance its expression. However, it is necessary to mention that he did not embrace the opposite extreme. It can be affirmed that he used Arabic words only when a Persian word did not exist, and when artistic purism would have been a clear disadvantage. His style does not preserve the language of the epic tradition; it is rather a living literary language, which, at his time, had already succeeded in being adopted by the ruling elite in prose literature. After him, it was impossible to return to such artificiality. He buried forever the old tradition and all those who imitated him later on followed the path he had laid out, although they were sometimes unable to comply with artistic norms.

If he reformed the language itself in this way, he also carried out no less essential reform of the techniques of epic poetry. Tradition required that any technical mastery would be developed mostly in lyrics belonging to the rhetorical genre. Epic as a narrative form was permitted to be poor in terms of expression. Hence court poetry was mostly hollow and cold. It was not narrating anything, it simply played with words, and if its technicality was removed, it would have been empty. Epics must first and foremost narrate something, but an unskilled poet cannot both narrate and play with words. Therefore, all the technical tricks of the ninth-century epic genre consisted mainly in lyric patterns, descriptions, digressions, etc.

To a certain extent Nizami followed this tradition, for his most elaborate and rhetorical language, of course, belongs to the descriptive passages, which are like elaborate carpets set into the fabric of the narrative. Nevertheless, he observed tradition only in part. He consistently followed a rule which required the highest artistic expressiveness, reaching the highest potential without damage to the train of thought embellished by every single verse. This is the reason for the complexity of his language, whose difficulty has been highlighted not only by European but also by Near Eastern critics. Nizami is difficult, yet the challenge is not similar to that presented by Khaqani for instance. Khaqani wrote intentionally difficult poems by using a wide range of scholastic expressions and comparisons that are inaccessible to the reader. His poems consist sometimes in cryptic depictions, but unfortunately, once the content of the *bayt* is deciphered, it is not worth the effort invested to understand it.

Nizami does not have such empty verses. Each of his difficult *bayts* can be understood and opens up for the reader a whole new world. In order to understand fully his poetry, the study of this form is absolutely necessary, it is only by weighing all the component parts of the verses, and by taking into account the various literary devices, that one can grasp his thoughts in all their depth. Hence one might say that each of Nizami's poems contains a double structure: in front of the reader is rolled out a grandiose canvas, full of actions with clearly and vividly described figures, and the classical precision typical of fables. This makes the whole appear as a harmonious unit. Beside this, however, each *bayt*, or sometimes pair of *bayt*s, acts as compositional whole, able to provide artistic pleasure outside its context. In other words, on the basic canvas is superimposed an infinite number of individual miniatures each of which is a unit.

One must not forget that Nizami imported this method from lyric poetry into epic, and moreover, that it became characteristic not only in literature, but also in the pictorial art of his time. Almost all bronze or porcelain objects of this period were given an aim in terms of composition, along with their basic function, as they were covered with ornamentation, often unrelated to the object, but still a part of the whole.

This artistry connects Nizami to a city where, at this time, figurative art was incredibly successful. This particular feature makes it possible to juxtapose him to the monumental tradition of aristocratic literature, where the centre of gravity is in the main narrative lines and the details are barely seen. Firdawsi's epic strives for the collective and for the suppression of individuality, while Nizami's poems are the successful resolution of the problems of the individual in a feudal context. Thus if one cannot obtain ones rights in real life, at least one can in Nizami's vivid depictions.

In order to render this short summary in a more convincing and accessible way to the reader who is not used to Nizami's original poetry, it is necessary to provide stylistic analyses of short extracts from *Khusraw and Shirin* in order to show more easily the complexity and the wealth of his writing style.

> *When night's musky ringlets were combed / The lamp of the day was transformed into a moth*
>
> *Beneath that ebony backgammon board, disappeared / Two dice, suffused arsenic-red*

The description occurs at night. In the first half of the verse, a parallel is drawn between the ringlets and the comb, in the second, between the lamp and the moth. In the second *bayt*, a combination of the names of the objects used to play backgammon is given. This is a particular technique. Now we shall turn to the images. The ringlets were combed, which spread out and hid the face full of light, like dusk enveloping the world. The sun, the light of the day, becomes a moth, i.e. it burned and ceased to exist, like the moth in the light of the candle. The freshness of the image lies in the fact that the light itself is transformed into a moth. The dice made of sandalwood are the golden sun, hidden by the dark wood in the obscurity of night sky. The *bayt* gives additional shade: the game ends, the backgammon is laid down...

> *Jupiter arose, a decree in hand / That freed the king*
> *from his bonds, and Shapur from affliction*

The depiction continues. Deep darkness arises and Jupiter becomes visible, according to the general astrological belief, this planet carries happiness and success. Jupiter's appearance here is a good omen. It announced a double release: the king, i.e. Khusraw, shall be freed from the shackles of a fruitless yearning for Shirin, and Shapur shall be freed from the woes of his roving and roaming and the potential retribution on his return if his assignment had not been fulfilled.

Here is another depiction of dawn:

> *When the spheres put on a ruddy cloak of squirrel fur,*
> *sewing up the rents in the sky / Night's black sable was*
> *hidden from the day's ermine*

The main purpose of the verses is clear: the author sets out the names of four animals with valuable fur. This is not simply a choice of words. The squirrel is also called the sinjab, it is a grey squirrel, and the choice of this animal serves as depiction for the sky, which is turning into the colour of ashes with the light. The sky rotates like the squirrel in a wheel, which is enhancing the comparison. The sable is an animal, the precise description of which cannot be given here. It has two colours, yellowish grey with white and coats are made out of its skin. This means, in other words, that the grey sky starts wearing a coat with white fringes, symbolising a glimmer of light on the horizon before dawn. The image is an extraordinarily expressive and concrete depiction of dawn.

Thousands such examples could be quoted, for verses of this kind are found many times on many pages, and one does not even need to look for them. Yet these serve as sufficient to illustrate Nizami's complexity. The images themselves can by no means be described as strained, or difficult to understand. Their complexity lies only in their succinctness, for there is one condition to their understanding: knowing all the details of life in this remote era. The first demand on the reader is not to turn away from concrete understandings, and not to imagine that they are a sort of cunning abstraction, but on the contrary, to remember that Nizami wanted first and foremost to give a palpable impression, to provide a visual, colourful image.

Yet it is a pity that we still do not possess enough knowledge about his times. There are no good dictionaries, as all of them are scanty and unreliable. The greatest help to decipher some complex comparisons might come from the poet himself, who used the same image in different places. Hence one might conclude that Nizami can be fully understood when a handbook of all of his works has been established, based on a critical edition of the texts, and each metaphor can be analysed in the light of historical data and the material culture of his time. This is an immense task, which is far beyond the strength of a single individual, requiring a whole institute, especially since the work cannot be limited to Azerbaijan: it necessitates parallel studies of Georgian and Armenian sources of the same period, having arisen in analogical historical conditions.

The verses cited are exemplary for one final reason: they highlight clearly the difficulties that Nizami represents for poetic translation. The translator does not have the right to limit himself to render in one way the idea of the verses. He must remember that the technicality of their design is an intrinsic part of Nizami's methodology. Consequently, he must by no means transfer Nizami's metaphors for our level of perception, but should preserve them exactly, which is of course an extremely difficult task considering Nizami's exceptional fertility of mind, for there is not always all the means in another language to express Nizami's conciseness and pithiness. Among all the translations produced so far, none has succeeded in this, no matter how close they were to rendering the beauty of the verses. Substantial work is required with many translators involved, and it should be added that they might only be counted as successful if they do not limit their work to the mechanical transfer of Nizami's text in a reformulated version, but try to study in depth the whole context of his times, to familiarise themselves with it and keep it constantly before their eyes.

Conclusion

The main elements which constitute Nizami's oeuvre have been covered as far as possible in this short survey. It is clear that only a small portion of the wealth of this work has been covered. A complete analysis of it would require more than a small book, probably ten volumes, which will undoubtedly be written at some point.

It is finally necessary to take stock and place Nizami within the history of world literature. It is impossible to examine here all potential questions. Only a limited number will be mentioned, and others require further study, in order to explore the endless wealth inherited by us from this great poet.

For greater clarity, the analysis is divided into three groups of questions: a) the social-societal significance of Nizami; b) his literary significance and c) the problem of influence. One should remember that these three groups are inseparable, for Nizami as a poet cannot be dissociated from Nizami as a social actor, hence this division, as mentioned above, serves only to provide a clearer outline of the selected questions.

First and foremost, this cursory survey of Nizami's poetry shows convincingly one of its characteristic features: the unbreakable link between Nizami and his home country, Azerbaijan. I use here this name, and not the term Arran, in which Ganja was located in the twelfth century, for Nizami himself refused to be contained within Arran's narrow boundaries, and to be fair, one should in fact include not only Azerbaijan but the whole Caucasus. This context is extremely important, because notwithstanding the language in which he wrote his oeuvre, Nizami preserved a distinct link with his homeland. Emblematic of this attitude is the way Nizami tried to bind the legends of Alexander to Azerbaijani soil. Following his particular love, he described the beauties of nature there. It is possible to say that the language is at its brightest when it comes to describe Barda'a, Tiflis and other cities of the Caucasus.

It should not be assumed, however, that Nizami understood 'homeland' in the current meaning of this word. In a feudal context without a national government, national feelings were only germinating as they did not have the conditions to develop. Nevertheless, the difference between Nizami and the feudal system had always been immense. In feudal understanding, there is no homeland. The feudal potentate feels well wherever he has power and can exploit the population. When he is attacked, he flees and finds another 'homeland', and if he defends anything, it will be his power only. Nizami, on the contrary, was already deeply aware of the need to protect one's homeland, the land which became fertile through the effort of one's grandfathers and great-grandfathers. The work of the people reinforces their rights to this land and this right must be preserved.

This position is reinforced by his clearly expressed hostility towards the main enemy of working people of the Caucasus: the Iranian ancestral aristocracy, striving to keep hold of these wealthy lands. Although Nizami leans on a tradition based in regions of prevailing Iranian culture, and although he admired the great genius of Firdawsi, he did not support the political theory of the Iranian aristocracy, as expressed in the *Shah-nama*. This is extremely important, for it shows that Nizami did not view Azerbaijan as part of Iran, and he decisively upheld its independence and freedom.

Notwithstanding all this, all chauvinist tendencies are completely alien to Nizami. We have noted the international character of the Azerbaijani cities of his times, and we have seen that the fratricidal strife which later appeared through the machinations of capitalism, were completely unknown at that time. In Nizami's view, a friend is whoever pursues the benefit of the working classes, while an enemy is whoever oppresses another, because nation, language and religion are not essential. In the poems analysed, numerous different peoples are described, from Russian to Indian and Chinese. Yet nowhere in Nizami's poetry do we find the idea that someone is bad because he is a representative of this or that nation.

Nizami's heroes originate from everywhere. The Iranian Bahram, the Arab Munzir, the Greek Alexander, are all good people. When they are upright and look after the prosperity of their people, there is no difference between them. This leads us to a fundamental driving motif that permeated all Nizami's output: his immense love for people, his outstanding humanism. Human beings in Nizami's view were the basis of everything, and its benefit decided everything. The good were those who brought benefit to the greatest number of others; the bad those who make people's existence in society unbearable. This illustrates the consistently negative attitude of Nizami towards violence which is so strongly expressed in almost all his poems. But at the same time Nizami was by no means in favour of non-resistance to evil. Evil should be opposed by all means, defending one's rights is an obligation.

One can deduce from this the role of the potentate, as personified by Alexander, who ought to be first and foremost the servant of the people. If he has rights to an individual life, it is only to the extent that his main purpose, i.e. serving his people, allows him. However, one might assume that Nizami did not hold necessary the presence of a higher authority for human society. At least, the dream of this 'blessed northern country' that he described in his last poem seems to express this idea clearly.

Nizami's characteristic respect for socially instrumental people is not limited to one half of them, that is the male half. Of course, Nizami does not talk about equal rights for women. It would be impossible to expect that in his time. Yet he recognises women's rights and that they were neither goods to be traded nor mere ornaments to life. On the contrary, they were the true companions and friends of men. The relationship between Nizami and the question of marriage, which is clearly exemplified in his personal life, is also in his poems (in a humorous form, though, in the seven tales of the *Seven Beauties*), for instance in the episode showing Alexander's care for the Kipchak women. We know very well how conquerors treated the women of conquered lands at that time and that for their hirelings they were a tasty prize of which no experienced general would think of depriving his soldiers of them. Alexander's behaviour thus seems dissonant here compared to the practices of the time. It is likely that Nizami did not believe that Alexander adopted such an attitude, but his concern lies not in what was done, but rather in that which should be done.

Almost all the literary scholars who have written about Nizami consider him by convention as an ascetic, living the life of a hermit, cut off from the world, staying in mystic exaltation. This short analysis seems to show quite convincingly that these interpretations are completely without foundation and ludicrous. It is true that Nizami took nothing or almost nothing for himself from this life. The lying and bombastic panegyrist was hateful to him, trading his intellect and ready to sell his unworthy soul for money. We do not know anything about his relationships with his countrymen or the role which he played among them. We have only his works to express his thoughts, and these speak clearly and eloquently. It shows the views that Nizami could have been defending in conversations with his intimates, the admonitions that he addressed to the rulers. While Nizami might not have performed any decisive actions, his words were those of a wise teacher and they called for progress, freedom, fraternity and a happy life. These very qualities of Nizami's may explain the fact that even though his name resonates within the Orient, and all authorities bow before him, the spread of his works is far from being sufficient. Some Timurid potentates from Central Asia vigorously spoke out against him in favour of his successor, Amir Khusraw, whose poems lacked any form of social concern and, despite all their entertaining construction and the beautiful external polish, they lack Nizami's immense moral strength.

In sum, Nizami, as a human being, as a social actor, was the bearer of the very best that was available in the twelfth century. His teaching is strong and severe, he does not make any allowances for people, but he follows his own path firmly believing in a better future. He does not seek to forget the fear of death in the hedonism of Omar Khayyam, nor does he agree to walk on the slavish path of the resourceful Sa'di. This is all understandable, for only such a great mind can establish everlasting value in art, for whoever has not suffered and burned in their soul will not find the words needed to express his thoughts.

* * *

Turning now to Nizami's contribution to world literature, it is first of notable significance that he succeeded in bringing together Western and Eastern traditions. One cannot deny that the contact which existed before Nizami between the Near East and the Antique world was stronger than is usually thought. In particular, it is almost impossible to answer successfully the question of the origin of Greek literature without taking into account the potential influence of Achaemenid authors. One should also remember that the Ghaznavid poet Unsuri (10-11th centuries) used Ancient Greek sources in one of his poems which has been preserved. Nevertheless, no one before Nizami had been in his position at the crossroads between the two cultures and benefitted from such unique possibilities. The esteem in which Nizami held Firdawsi has already been highlighted. Yet for all that, attributing the birth of his poem to the *Shah-nama,* as has been common until now, is misguided. Parallel to the heroic epic, the Near East succeeded in developing already in the tenth century some local epic forms, which can be compared with the chivalric romances of the Middle Ages. Nizami's work is based upon this kind of poetry, but one cannot describe his poems as chivalric romances. While *Khusraw and Shirin* contains the main motif of the "knight's chivalrous courtship", this is not the core of the poem. Nizami's task is to demonstrate how to change the destiny of his heroes through all the characteristics of their personality. In other words, instead of replicating stock characters, Nizami tries to individualise, to build psychological characteristics, which are totally foreign to chivalric romances. Consider the famous "Vis and Ramin" by Fakhr al-Din Gurgani, it represents a well-known attempt in this direction, even though the author was incapable of showing the personality of the hero. As for Nizami, he broke with the framework of epic poetry and replaced it with romantic poetry. After him, it was impossible to return to ancient tradition, and all the later attempts like the *Timur-nama*, *Shahinshah-nama*, etc. use dead, worn out patterns, and thus exhibit a pseudo-classical imitative character.

His deep psychological analysis, the product of his extraordinary knowledge of the human soul allowed Nizami to establish a whole series of classic heroic types, who became part of the world treasury of literature. The examples of Shirin Farhad, Layla and Majnun, Bahram, and Alexander were given their definitive shape by Nizami. From then on, it was in this guise that the whole literature of the Near East was inspired by them, from Turkey to Muslim India; they live on in the present and will live forever. Authors after Nizami tried to reinterpret their characters, showing them in a different light, but almost none of them succeeded in reshaping them significantly.

What is more, these figures have entered folklore and become accessible on the widest scale, still, of course, under the direct influence of Nizami. This is a tremendously important fact, for we should remember that spreading written works among an overwhelmingly illiterate population was exceptionally difficult until the great socialist October Revolution. Only such a powerful mastery, combined with a profound love for people could overcome this difficulty. In this regard, the exceptional diffusion of his brilliance can be counted as a clear sign of his immense social value. Yet beside the fact that Nizami influenced the folklore of a wide range of peoples, he was himself reciprocally interested in folklore. It should be noted here that folklore has always been denigrated in literary circles in the Near East. A sharp division forced the intelligentsia of feudal society, which mainly comprised the ruling class, to disregard folklore, and to turn to themes developed in sophisticated 'higher social spheres'. This created an impoverishment of this type of literature, was expressed in ossification and formulaic play, characteristic of some authors of the Timurid period.

By virtue of his social position and his suspicion of relations with the authorities, Nizami did not consider it useful to follow traditions. The stories in *Seven Beauties*, some episodes of the *Iskandar-nama* and the main narratives in *Makhzan al-Asrar*, contain clear links to folkloric themes. Nizami, especially in his stories, adopted the approach of the popular storytellers, with its characteristic devices and themes, and achieved extraordinary results. He demonstrated how to compose lively literature and only those poets who can and are willing to accept this path succeed in achieving such powerful results. After all, it is not accidental that in the numerous imitations of the *Seven Beauties* the most lively and interesting parts are the stories in which successive authors introduced new themes.

Nizami's decisive reform in the structure of poetry led, so to speak, to the canonisation by him of a certain type of romantic poetry. Nizami highlighted three aspects of love: heroic love (Khusraw Farhad Shirin), tragic, catastrophic love (Layla and Majnun), and the whimsical light playful love (*The Seven Beauties*, which contains a wide range of different shades). Each of these aspects is linked to a particular poetic metre, as mentioned above. These metres remained linked once and for all to that type of poem for all of the peoples, who adopted the Arabo-Persian metrical system. We can categorically affirm that working on a theme similar to *Layla and Majnun* using the metre of *Khusraw and Shirin* has been inconceivable throughout the past eight hundred years. This shows how wide Nizami's influence is and how strong his proficiency in literature was, because each metre must now necessarily be used in one specific way. It is absolutely clear that it was Nizami who imprinted their character and coloration on them, as before him no clear tradition seems to have been established.

Thus Nizami established a poetic canon for the Oriental epic tradition. And if in the end the preservation of this canon throughout eight centuries and its use by hack poets, combined with unfavourable social conditions led, in the sixteenth and seventeenth centuries, to lamentable results, the blame cannot be laid on Nizami. His works have been imitated endlessly, yet only the greatest authors should have the right to imitate him, and therefore it does not come as a surprise that many of these imitations give the impression not of copies, but caricatures.

As for language reform, it does not seem necessary to repeat here that which has been said above. Yet, one crucial point must be added at this stage. It has been stated that Nizami shattered tradition, and that, finding it shackled by the language of his time, he revived and enriched it: in short, he modernized it. But surely from this step, there follows a logical sequence of steps leading to the inevitable conclusion of rejection of the Persian language as the only language of communication. Although we do not have any works by Nizami in another language, nevertheless the ground for rejection of this language was nonetheless prepared by the poet himself. The potential for this already existed, but implementing it would have required more decisive changes in the interactions of Near Eastern peoples. This shock was provided by the Mongols who signalled the advent of the collapse of the Iranian tradition. The floodgates were opened, and that for which the preparations had already been made rapidly took place.

The question of Nizami's influence upon his successors has already been raised several times. With some words regarding this topic we will conclude this last chapter. I insist that it is in fact impossible to exhaust this topic. To name here all Nizami's successors, would require a full literary history of the Near East. It should be said firstly that research on Nizami's influence has not even started yet as it is an immense work and for each of the sections of the *khamsa*, a solid thirty to forty printed page monograph could be written.

The imitations of Nizami's works already started during the poet's lifetime, and looked like shameless plagiarism more than anything else. The poet talked abundantly about this in almost all his compositions. None of these early works have survived, probably because they did not have enough artistic quality, but at the beginning of the thirteenth century, a whole series of authors made systematic attempts to reproduce the *Khamsa*, the component parts of which had already gone up to seven in the fifteenth century (Jami, Zulali). The first imitators hardly changed the names, adding sometimes a simple inversion like Shirin and Khusraw or Majnun and Layla. Later, the heroes' names started being modified, but their fundamental character was preserved.

European literature specialists would usually call such imitations, providing they were written not in Persian but in another language, a translation. But the fact that the vast majority of these works were written in Persian makes it inaccurate to call them 'translations'. In the East, in fact, they were designated with the term *nazira*, i.e. a reply or competitor. Preserving the metre and the most important points, every author reworked the sections inbetween. Clearly, if an author was original and talented, the *nazira* can represent extremely high artistic value, if he was an imitator then the result was only sad scribblings.

Among those who imitated Nizami, it is worth mentioning such poets as Amir Khusraw Dehlavi (1253-1325), Salman Savaji (d. 1377), Abd al-Rahman Jami (1414-1492), Khatifi (d. 1521), who all wrote in Persian. In the Golden Horde in the fourteenth century, a text in Kipchak language was created and called *The Book of Khusraw and Shirin*. In the Central Asian Turkic language, a *Khamsa* was created by the Uzbek merchant and great literary writer, Mir Alisher Navoli (1441-1503). In the Azerbaijani language, the great poet Fuzuli (d. 1562) is best known for his beautiful version of *Layla and Majnun*.

Beside these literary imitations and remakes, the number of which has reached several dozens, Nizami's heroes are to be found in the folklore of Azerbaijan, Georgia, Armenia, Iran, Turkey, Kurdistan, Turkmenistan, Uzbekistan and Tajikistan, to name but a few. Hence we can safely affirm that Nizami's heroes became particularly appreciated among the masses, even more than Homer's famous heroes, the study of which was inculcated among all in Europe for centuries. The folklore of these peoples lives until now. Among those of them who had the good fortune to enter the fraternal family of the Soviet Union, it continues to be enriched and grow day by day, and Nizami's heroes live on to this day without having lost any of their fascinating power.

Nizami's Alexander was looking for the source of eternal life in the land of darkness, but he did not find it. The great poet found the Water of Life, through the charm of his powerful creative words which gave his heroes life and eternal youth.

Nizami knew well the immense force of words and he knew that words created by great masters fear neither the dust of centuries, nor the vicissitudes of historical destiny. We can only adhere to the proud words of this famous poet, the truth of which has been confirmed by history itself:

> *While there is speech, may it be spoken of / May speech revitalise Nizami's name*

Notes

1. V.M. Molotov, *Tretii pyatiletnii plan razvitii narodnogo xozyaistva SSSR. Doklad i zaklyuchitel'noe slovo na XVIII s¢ezde VKP(b)*, OGIZ, 1939, p. 62.
2. acc. to EI2 Jamāl al-Dīn Abū Muḥammad Ilyās b. Yūsuf b. Zakī Mu'ayyad
3. Afẓal al-Dīn Bādil Ibrāhīm ibn 'Alī Khāqānī Shīrvānī
4. A Turkish city in the province of Kars, south of the Armenian border.
5. The exact date is impossible to determine, it could have been anywhere between 1167 and 1174.
6. The English translation is from Ibn Batuta, *A.D. 1325-1354. Volume 2 Translated... by H.A.R. Gibb*. Cambridge, published for the Hakluyt Society at the University Press, 1962, pp. 418-421.
7. The Georgian translation of the poem *Khusraw and Shirin* apparently dates back to the fourteenth century.
8. It is true that in Sanai's poetry one will encounter many verses dedicated to the ruling elite, but on the whole, they do not occupy a predominant position.

9. This is a historical figure. His actual name most probably. To his son, Katus, was attributed the construction of Ta-i Bustan in Kermanshah. Khavarnak have been preserved.
10. The poet gives their names: Furek, Nazperi, Azeriun, and Dursiti.
11. Which matches the alternation of black and white.
12. However, Arran under Rus. They conquered Barda'a and stayed there for a relatively long period in 946/7.